THE ONE GOD

FOUNDATIONS OF CATHOLIC THEOLOGY SERIES

Gerard S. Sloyan, *Editor*

THE ONE GOD

WILFRID F. DEWAN, CSP

St. Paul's College
Washington, D.C.

PRENTICE-HALL, INC.
Englewood Cliffs, N.J.

1963

Nihil Obstat:

John F. Harvey, OSFS
Censor Deputatus

Imprimatur:

✠ Patrick A. O'Boyle, DD
Archbishop of Washington
October 3, 1962

PRENTICE-HALL INTERNATIONAL, INC., *London*
PRENTICE-HALL OF AUSTRALIA, PTY., LTD., *Sydney*
PRENTICE-HALL OF CANADA, LTD., *Toronto*
PRENTICE-HALL FRANCE, S.A.R.L., *Paris*
PRENTICE-HALL OF JAPAN, INC., *Tokyo*
PRENTICE-HALL DE MEXICO, S.A., *Mexico City*

C

EDITOR'S NOTE

This series offers the depth and richness of the divine message of salvation proclaimed to us by Christ. The theology, or "faith seeking understanding" contained here is not on a catechetical level, nor yet on a complex, higher level; it is clear and nontechnical, but at the same time adult and thorough. It is a scholarly presentation of revelation.

These volumes do not adopt an apologetic approach. They

neither attempt to justify Catholic faith nor aim at convincing those who do not profess it of the reasonableness of believing. This series is written primarily for those who already believe, who accept the Church as the living continuation of Christ, and the Scriptures as divinely inspired.

The authors do not attempt a philosophy of God or of Christianity, but a study of the mystery of God seen through the eyes of faith. The mystery of faith will not be dispelled by the study of these books. It will remain.

Since some background in philosophy on the part of the reader is needed, and cannot in every case be presumed, there are times when philosophical terms will need to be explained. Philosophical reasoning is very much a part of speculative theology.

Although the breakdown of the series is along traditional lines, each volume is designed to emphasize the oneness of God's plan of salvation and not its different facets. Distinction is made in order to unite. What is taught in the Scriptures is stressed, so that it may be seen how men of the Bible understood the message entrusted to them. The historical aspects of doctrine as held by Christians are then treated: the testimony of the early Christian writers and the liturgy to the belief of the Church; the controversies and heresies that necessitated defense and precise formulation, and finally, the magisterial teaching in each subject area. In this way speculative theology, or the present understanding of each mystery, is not seen in isolation from the sources of faith.

Thus, the revealed Christian message is viewed as the *tradition* (in the fullest and best sense of that theological term) expressed in and through the Church over the centuries—more explicitly formulated, from age to age, and with further applications. But it is still the same saving message begun in the Old Testament and perfected in the mystery and person of Jesus Christ.

One last point is important. Although the study of theology is an exercise of intellect, it can never be exclusively this. The message of Jesus Christ is a living Word, an invitation to participate in the saving event of the redemption, starting in this world by faith and the union of grace, and culminating in heaven by vision and immediate union. This invitation demands response or living faith. The study of the Christian message through theology requires such response, for the message is not something that was heard and assented to once. It is a Word addressed to us that requires our vigorous "Yes" for a lifetime.

CONTENTS

INTRODUCTION TO THEOLOGY, *page* 3

*Christ, the fullness of God's saving message.
The Church, continuation of the saving
message. Development of the message.
Faith, the acceptance of the message. Theology, the exposition and understanding of
the message. Selected readings.*

vii

THE ONE GOD

CHAPTER ONE

THE EXISTENCE OF GOD, *page 35*

God's path to us: revelation. Man's path to God: created things.

CHAPTER TWO

WHAT GOD IS, *page 59*

The scriptural picture of God. Theological clarifications on the nature of God. Clarifications regarding our knowledge of God.

CHAPTER THREE

GOD'S ACTIVITY, *page 81*

Divine knowledge. Divine volition. Providence, salvific will, predestination. Creation.

SELECTED READINGS, *page 105*

Chapters One–Three.

ABBREVIATIONS, *page 107*

INDEX, *page 109*

INTRODUCTION
TO THEOLOGY

JESUS CHRIST, THE FULLNESS OF REVELATION

"I am the way, and the truth, and the life. No one comes to the Father but through me." (Jn 14,6)

"All things have been created through and unto him, and he is before all creatures, and in him all things hold together." (Col 1,16f)

(Fresco in the Catalonian Chapel. Courtesy, Museum of Fine Arts, Boston)

INTRODUCTION
TO THEOLOGY

Theology is intimately linked with God's revelation, his saving message. Only if seen in this context will it take on real vitality and importance, no matter how interesting it may be intellectually apart from this central consideration. Our first task, then, is to point out the relationship between the science of theology and the message of salvation.

CHRIST,
THE FULLNESS OF GOD'S SAVING MESSAGE

In the Old Testament God began his self-revelation to men. Through the prophets and his constant intervention in favor of the chosen race, he initiated his plan of salvation. What helped to distinguish this religion from all others was the intimacy and familiarity God invited. He revealed himself as a person; he set up a personal, an "I-Thou" relationship with his people. But God expected an answer, a response of faith and love to such generosity. The Old Testament is nothing but the account of this ever more explicit message of God and of the response made by his people.

God's plan of salvation was only partially revealed to the people of Israel. The fullness of the message came only with and in Jesus Christ. The divine Word, second person of the Trinity, took flesh and came upon earth to bring us the full message, the good news of salvation, and to bring to completion the eternal plan hidden in God. Indeed, revelation is not to be identified merely with a set of truths *about* God which the Church must hold, but with the very work and person of Christ himself. For Christ and his message are both *the Word of God*. St. Paul writes: "It was little by little and in different ways that God spoke in olden times to our forefathers through the prophets, but in these latter days he has spoken to us in a Son, whom he destined to possess everything, through whom he has made the world." (Heb 1,1f)

In the Old Testament God made himself felt as a living presence through his actions; all the more is this true when he comes to us in Christ, the embodiment of the "mystery of God" by which he wills to save us. Christ in his life, death, resurrection, and glorification not only brings us salvation but *is* salvation, the saving event; he is the embodiment and fulfillment of the plan of salvation begun so long before.

If we understand our Lord as the personal self-giving of God, as the great saving event in himself, we can see why he is the fullness of revelation and why we await no further public revelation. In giving us the Word Incarnate, his perfect image, the Father can give us no more.

4

THE CHURCH,
CONTINUATION OF THE SAVING MESSAGE

Salvation for the followers of the earthly Christ lay in the personal acceptance of him, and response to him and the message of salvation; briefly, in coming into responsive contact with the Word of God (which term includes the notion of Christ as person, as saving event, as fullness of revelation). But how do we, living so long after, enjoy this chance; how do we come into contact with Christ and his message? For Protestant Christians, in general, it was (and is) through the Bible. However, this is only a partial answer: there is more to be said.

Christ prolonged his presence and message for us by fashioning a Church to which he entrusted this saving message. Another volume will show how this Church is the body of Christ, a vital, living thing, throbbing with the same life and Spirit of Christ. Salvation for us still comes by personal contact with him and his saving message, but *through* and *in* his Church. How the Church embodies this Word of God, this message, will appear in the following sections.

Tradition, the Lived Message

Revelation ended with Christ (or at least with the death of the last apostle, the last of the specially appointed eyewitnesses of Christ). But nothing was to be lost. He entrusted his message and saving work to a Church founded upon the apostles. He sent them out to all nations to preach the message of salvation. There was to be a transmission, a handing over of this unchangeable but ever-living Word of God. From this comes the word "tradition" (from *tradere*, to hand over). Apostolic tradition is precisely this total message of salvation to be passed on to all mankind. It is not something inert, mere facts, but a living reality. Just as the Word of God was alive and life-giving because embodied in Christ and inseparable from him, so tradition, this identical Word of God, is alive and life-giving because embodied in the mystical body of Christ, his Church.

The first transmission of the gospel message, the good news (another way to say in English the Greek word *euaggelion*, gospel) was by oral preaching; the words were given deeper meaning and vigor by the way in which the Christian community was taught to respond in worship and action. Briefly, by the will of Christ his Church took on the very life and message and saving activity of Christ himself. In and through the Church Christ continues his saving message for all time. We cannot insist too much that this handed-on message, namely tradition, is not something outside the Church, but possessed, lived, and preached by the Church herself.

Again, just as revelation, the Word of God in Christ, embraced the content of the message and the actions by which our Lord revealed, so too tradition, the Word of God in the Church, embraces both the passive sense of the totality of the saving message transmitted, and the action by which the Church transmits it to all generations. Many theologians today speak of tradition as the here-and-now consciousness the Church has of the Christian message, or again, as the "memory" of the Church—embracing both what is remembered and the active power of judging, perceiving, and transmitting the message.

It would be absurd to think that mere men—and the Church is made up of men—could faithfully pass on this message without distortion. But when these men are members of the mystical body of Christ which is animated by the Holy Spirit, the Spirit of truth, then such is possible. Every one of the faithful is meant to be a witness proclaiming this message; none can be completely passive in the communication of the message. Since, however, one or even many could be mistaken about the content and implications of the message, thinking their own inspirations to be those of the Spirit, Christ wisely provided his Church with official teachers: the apostles in the early Church and the bishops today, among whom the Roman bishop or pope has a place of eminence as teacher. This "teaching Church" (*magisterium*) is the one, official, and infallible mouthpiece of tradition or the Word of God.

Sources of the Message: Bible and Apostolic Traditions

6   The lived message, at first preached orally, was soon committed to writing under direct inspiration. Under the impulse and direction of

the Holy Spirit, Matthew, Mark, and Luke (the synoptic authors, so called) set down in print the current oral proclamation of the saving message, their inspired remembrances of Christ's life and teaching. The Acts of the Apostles are a brief history of the early life of the Church, her proclamation and teaching, as she began to live and spread the gospel. The writings of St. Paul and later St. John represent a more advanced stage in the understanding of the same message. Thus the New Testament is the tradition, or the Church's consciousness of the Word of God, in written form.

But is the totality of the Christian message found in Scripture? This is a delicate and much debated question today among Catholics. The Council of Trent (1548-1563) tells us that the whole message promulgated by Christ and to be preached to every creature is contained "in written books *and in the unwritten* [i.e., extra-Scriptural] *traditions* that the apostles received from Christ himself or that were handed on, as it were from hand to hand [person to living person] from the apostles under the inspiration of the Holy Spirit, and so have come down to us." (D783)

Now first of all, what are these unwritten traditions? They refer to ways of Christian worship and living established by Christ or the apostles under the inspiration of the Holy Spirit. The apostles certainly wrote down the heart of the message, but besides this there were the oral formulae, actions, judgments, decisions, interpretations, customs, liturgical practices; in short, the gospel message as expressed for example in infant baptism, prayers for the dead, and administration of sacraments. These, too, were external embodiments of the message as much as was the Bible, hence "sources" of the message. (To avoid confusing these with tradition as mentioned above, we always refer to them in the plural—as did the Council—and with a mental small "t".) Note that these apostolic traditions have to do with essential faith and morals, and are not to be confused with ecclesiastical traditions, which can come and go in the life of the Church (e.g., communion under one species, priestly celibacy, pious customs and practices).

Now back to our question: what is the relationship between these two objective sources of the Christian message, Scripture and apostolic traditions? Does each contain a part of the total message? The Council of Trent did not decide the question. But sixteenth-century Protestant

7

emphasis on Scripture *alone* led many Catholic writers subsequent to Trent to assert that the two were complementary sources: hence their formula "partly-partly." Subsequently, the majority came to hold that all revelation is contained in the apostolic traditions, and part of it (indeed most) is recorded in some radical fashion in Scripture: "wholly-partly," then. Today, however, a growing number of theologians of weight are coming around to what is considered the position before Trent, namely that all revelation is contained, at least essentially or substantially, in Scripture. Thus, when the Bible is read *in* and *by* the Church, to which it belongs after all, the fullness of the message of Christ can be found therein: "wholly-wholly," therefore.

Without trying to decide this important issue, if we see revelation as the unfolding of the mystery of Christ, as a living whole, as one unified plan of salvation, there are many reasons for considering Scripture, which confronts us with the person of Christ and his plan of salvation, as transmitting to us the totality of the Word of God. But again, it does so only when read *in* and *by* the Church, whose writings the Scriptures are.

Thus, in brief, tradition (or apostolic tradition) is the continuing and ever-living total message of Christ as lived by the Church, whereas the Bible and apostolic traditions (or institutions) are the objective sources or organs of the message.

Church or Scripture?

The question arises, how can the Church presume to judge the inspired Word of God in Scripture? Such is the basic difficulty of the Protestant. Oscar Cullman admits the prior existence of an oral apostolic tradition as taught and lived by the infant Church, but sees the work of the apostles as unique. He does not think their role or infallibility was passed on to the later Church; rather the Church herself, about 150 A.D., seeing the danger of alterations of her doctrine, made a great act of humility when it fixed the canon of Scripture, and made it from that time on the ultimate criterion of the integrity of her belief and action. She humbly submits herself to the Word of God in Scripture. Cullman is convinced that the Catholic Church by not admitting this is judging apostolic tradition by post-apostolic traditions, that is, the

8

Word of God by later ecclesiastical accretions. (See "Scripture and Tradition" in *Christianity Divided,* pp. 7-29.)

But Catholics hold that it is precisely the apostolic tradition as taught by the apostles, hence the full message of Christ, the pure Word of God, which is embodied in the life and consciousness of the Church. The Bible, to be sure, is also the Word of God, and is cherished as the uniquely inspired written expression of this same message; it remains for the Church the clearest source of the Word. But it is the same Word of God in both cases.

What Cullman fails to see is that the Word of God continues to live in all its fullness and purity within the Church—not because of the fallible human beings who are its members, but rather in spite of them; the reason it does so is that the Church is the mystical body of Christ, animated with the same life and Spirit as Christ himself. Cullman fails to see that the promise of infallibility given to the apostles is as real for the teaching Church today as it was for them.

For this reason, the Catholic theologians who insist that the total message is contained in Scripture immediately add that its implications can only be clearly seen when this written Word of God is interpreted by the *living* Word of God that encompasses it, namely tradition. Thus, tradition is *not something other than Holy Scripture* and added to it, but rather the entire living transmission of the truth, whose central organ is the inspired Scripture. It keeps its true and complete sense only when it remains a vital part of that living tradition of the Church in which the inspired writers actually composed it, making it, as it were, the essential deposit of this tradition. (See L. Bouyer, *The Word, Church and Sacraments,* pp. 53f.)

So, there can be no question about which is greater. It is the same Word of God in each case. The fact is that the Church possesses the Word both in lived *and* written form. Far from changing it or claiming superiority, her one aim is to preserve, develop, and proclaim the Word of God.

DEVELOPMENT OF THE MESSAGE

Besides guarding and preaching the message of salvation, the Church of Christ must also explain, clarify, and develop it. Hence the

9

development of doctrine or dogma. A dogma is a truth contained in the original revelation and infallibly presented to the faithful to be believed (D1792). It is undeniable that Catholics today believe many more dogmas than formerly. For example, the eunuch converted by Philip was only required to profess faith in Jesus Christ as Son of God. (Ac 8,37) The creeds were later and fuller formulations of this faith in Christ; today we have still other defined doctrines such as Mary's immaculate conception in her mother's womb.

Far from being unfaithful to the original message, however, no one is more careful than the Church not to innovate. While keeping the message intact, the Church constantly strives to show more clearly the beauty and content of revelation. Unchangeableness and development are in no way incompatible. Even in early times the necessity of both was recognized. Vincent of Lérins wrote, "Therefore, let there be growth . . . and all possible progress in understanding, knowledge, and wisdom whether in single individuals or in the whole body, in each man as well as in the entire Church, according to the stage of their development; but only within proper limits, that is, in the same doctrine, in the same meaning, and in the same purport." (A Commonitory, n. 28) Both we and the early Christians believe the same amount of truth, the same total message of Christ; but we more explicitly, more in detail than they.

In explaining why we have more dogmas today, two notions are to be avoided. The first implies that the early Church had no more than the germ or seed of the message, which grew into a mighty oak. This underplays the fullness of the message possessed from the beginning. The second theory exaggerates, saying that everything was perfectly clear and explicit, but often passed along from mouth to mouth without being recorded anywhere. This theory would see the dying Peter whispering to Linus, his successor, ". . . and she was assumed into heaven, but of course there is no need to publicize this since the whole community knows it."

Just how clear then was Christ's message to the apostles and the early Church? First, the unique case of the apostles: the Lord Jesus communicated the whole message to them not only in words but by his whole life: every action and attitude (e.g., toward sin, Peter's leadership, his virgin mother, etc.) lent added meaning to what he said.

They not only heard the message, but "experienced" it on every level of their personalities, till the mystery of Christ filled them to overflowing. As the very pillars of the Church they were undoubtedly given special insights, until they possessed a fuller awareness of the total message than will ever again be achieved, though not in the explicit formulas or dogmas later theology would bring about.

After Pentecost their whole lives were consumed with the effort to bring this message to others, to bring others into living contact with Christ in his newly established Church. Before death overcame them they succeeded in embodying this living message in the very life and worship of the Church, and in committing at least the essence of it to inspired writings. What the Church possessed at that point was the fullness of revelation to which nothing can be added, for the apostles handed over to the infant Church the message and even the "experience" of Christ. Since their heirs were men who had not experienced Christ and did not have special "lights," the task these men had of coming to an explicit understanding of the message was all the greater. But circumstances, love, and especially the action of the Holy Spirit have brought about a gradual formulation and explication of the content of this lived message.

We must now speak of two different ways in which the message can develop or become more explicit. The first involves a *logical* unfolding of further truths from propositions clearly contained in the message. On the one hand there can be continually improving, that is to say, clearer statements of the *same* truth. For example, we need only compare the clarity of the Council of Florence's formula of the Trinity with that of Nicea. In theory this could go on forever, since no human formula can ever encompass a divine mystery or exhaust its content. On the other hand we can arrive at *new* truths implicit in already clearly stated dogmas, just as the idea of freedom is implicit in the knowledge of what human nature is. In this way, from the revealed fact that Jesus is true God and true man there can be deduced (though not all like this term) the fact that he has both a human intellect and a human will. Theologians speak of such truths as being formally (immediately) implicit in revelation and able to be defined as new dogmas.

Sometimes human logic can only arrive at a high degree of fittingness; for example, Mary's motherhood of the God-man, her sinlessness, her fullness of grace, and so on, make her assumption very likely (some would say even necessary). In any case, is it not possible for the teaching Church under the special light of the Holy Spirit to see, by a "supernatural logic," in such a convergence of probable arguments the implicitly revealed truth of Mary's bodily assumption?

Not all development of dogma can be explained in terms of logic, however, if indeed any can. Man is far from being a pure intellect, and much more is involved in the growth and enrichment of any doctrine than mere logic. Think of all the events and experience that have gone into our fuller understanding of the notions of liberty and democracy. Thus we must take account of another way in which dogma can grow, a *vital*, living way.

Cardinal Newman likened Christianity or the message of salvation to a great idea passed on by some genius to posterity—not any kind of idea, such as that two and two is four, but a *vital* one like liberty, or equality, which "involves" us personally, touches us in every fiber of our being. Now the apostles grasped the idea of Christ with a never-to-be-surpassed clarity—even though they did not formulate it in terms of later theology. They had to pass it on to men not so enlightened as they. If by the nature of the human mind time is necessary for the full comprehension and perfection of great ideas, all the more is this true of the mind's mastery of the highest truths. Even though given to the world once for all by inspired teachers, these truths could not be understood all at once by the early Christians. Since the message had to be transmitted in human words and to noninspired minds, all the more time and deeper thought was necessary for its elucidation. (See J. H. Newman, *An Essay on the Development of Christian Doctrine*, pp. 53-63.)

Newman's insight into the possibility of grasping the whole Christian message even from the beginning, but as an "idea" still imperfectly understood, is very valuable. For then it is possible to say that doctrines such as the immaculate conception and the assumption of the Mother of God are not believed because defined, but defined because they have always been believed. If Christians have always believed them, it is precisely because they sensed obscurely, unreflexively, instinctively, that they were contained in the other truths of the deposit of revelation,

12

and were demanded by the totality of Christian doctrine. (See C. Journet, "Scripture and the Evolution," in *The Dogma of the Immaculate Conception*, p. 17.)

Can real knowledge be present to our consciousness (or that of the Church) without being clearly seen for a time? It would seem that the answer is yes. Take the example of children whose parents have passed on whole family traditions to them, not only in word but by their example and whole life. Children, who are wonderfully observant, drink all these in—but largely in a "global," unreflected way. Only later, when they begin to mature and reflect—especially if they have loved their parents deeply—do they begin to see the fullness of what was truly passed on to them. "Now I see what mother meant when she told me that."

One more example may help. The boy who falls deeply in love undergoes a tremendous experience. He is aware of this love in every fiber of his being, and it surpasses anything he can say about it. Yet a gifted lover can slowly, haltingly, find a way to express this love to himself, to his fiancée, and to others. In fact if he did not think about it, express it, it would soon begin to fade. Reflection and expression actually help to preserve his experience. They even cause him to see depths to which he did not perhaps advert in the beginning.

We have already mentioned how the apostles had a tremendous, overwhelming "experience" of Christ and his message. They did not therefore bequeath to the Church a set of propositions only; under the guidance of the Holy Spirit they left the Church this vital experience of the message, or of their encounter with Christ. Certainly this experience is related in inspired words by the Bible, but it can only be fully captured by *living* this experience in and through the Church.

These examples do not do justice to the unfolding of the message of Christ. If it is possible for the gifted parent or lover to communicate a total experience, through inadequate words, to a sympathetic and completely "attuned" listener, how much the more is this true in the case of the Church itself. For the message and total experience of Christ are not being handed down and gradually formulated by totally distinct people, but transmitted to successive generations of Christians who themselves are intimately bound together as parts of the one living body of Christ on earth. This Church can truly be said to have a collective

13

consciousness or awareness of the message, particularly (as will be seen in the volume on the Church) when we realize that it really lives by the life of Christ himself, under the influence and infallible guidance of the Holy Spirit.

Many factors can play a role in causing the Church to look more deeply into the message or to formulate it more precisely.

(a) One is the challenge of heresy. When Arius denied that the Son is like the Father in *ousía,* the Council of Nicea in 325 A.D. had to affirm it in clear terms. Often the development will already have taken place within the Church; the heresy is only an occasion to put it into words.

(b) Theological reflection has likewise often led to a deeper grasp of the content of our faith, for example, St. Augustine's theology of grace, and the scholastics' work on the sacraments.

(c) The piety of the faithful can be the expression in worship of truths of faith. This certainly played a role with regard to the definition of the assumption. The Holy Spirit sees to it that false devotions do not take root, or soon die out, while genuine ones blossom.

(d) Liturgical life, though born of dogma, can contribute to it also. Dogma and liturgy leap beyond one another at times; an example would be the reciprocal relationship between the early Church's prayers for the dead and the doctrine of purgatory.

(e) Finally and most important of all is the role of the teaching Church, the *magisterium.* This agency of the Spirit does not always initiate doctrinal progress, but it always observes, guides, and judges it. The final guarantee of true development lies uniquely with this teaching Church. For only the bishops in union with the pope, or the pope alone, are divinely protected by infallibility in deciding once for all that a certain doctrine is truly a part of the divine revelation.

In short, then, development of doctrine does not mean new revelation. Neither does it mean that the message of Christ has grown or changed. It is simply the more explicit and clearer formulation of the Church's awareness of the "Christian idea" or message of salvation, which was communicated to her once in its fullness through the apostles. This comprehension which the Church has of divine revelation is called upon to go ever deeper, until the Church and all its members "attain

14

to the deep knowledge of the Son of God . . . and to the mature measure of the fullness of Christ." (Eph 4,13)

FAITH, THE ACCEPTANCE OF THE MESSAGE

Through revelation God offers us not just knowledge about himself, but a whole new relationship with him. Even in the Old Testament it is clear that God is entering into a personal self-giving to men. In the New Testament, when God becomes incarnate in Jesus Christ, this total gift of God to us is all the more evident, for he comes to us not merely in word and deed, but in his own Son.

This self-giving, this revelation, is not meant to be a one-way street, a monologue. A response or answer is expected. The prophets saw the urgent need for this response in terms of accepting and living the message of God. Nor for the apostles was the reply to the self-giving of Christ in words alone but in the wholehearted acceptance of him and his message, a total dedication or commitment of their beings to him. This can be summed up in the word *faith,* which is the acceptance of the message, the living answer given by man to the God who came in Christ.

The Full Notion of Faith

FAITH AS AN ENCOUNTER WITH CHRIST   If we see faith as a total commitment, a full acceptance of Christ and his message, then faith is also an *encounter*. It is a living answer, a whole attitude of life. This is what it meant to the men of the New Testament. Nor has the situation changed for us. Revelation is no mere fact, but ultimately a person. Our response, then, is not to a fact but to a person.

We still encounter Christ, and God in Christ. Christianity is still as much a personal thing, an "I-Thou" relationship, as it was for those who believed in the visible Christ. The early converts of the apostles were not merely told about Christ, but were led to encounter him through an intimate message-response, made possible precisely because Christ and his saving message and work remain present in his Church. *15* We today are invited to this same personal encounter with Christ in his Church. For the Church is not a wall between us and Christ, not even a mediator or go-between; rather, it is the meeting ground. More precisely, the Church is the union of us and Christ. The Word of God (message and person of Christ) is found within his Church. The Mass and other sacraments are not just images of what he did but extensions of his saving actions. We, as much as the apostles and early Christians, are still being invited to direct contact with the saving mysteries of Christ's life, death, and resurrection.

Thus faith is not mere belief in a Jesus of long ago, but a vital here-and-now existential encounter with Christ. Living faith makes him as real and influential in our lives today as he was for his closest followers. Faith must have this *here-and-nowness*. It is not an act we can make once and then sit back satisfied. It must be a living movement toward God who invites us by his message and draws us by his grace.

FAITH AS TOTAL COMMITMENT   The good mother who gives herself unselfishly to her children deserves their *complete faith,* that is, acceptance of what she says, trust, confidence, hope, conviction, love, obedience. In short, it means total commitment to her as a person. And this is the faith of the true Christian. This is the faith of the martyr—whether under Nero or the Communists—who dies "for the faith," that is, because of his deep, personal engagement to Christ.

Only in this full sense do all the various meanings of faith which we find in Scripture meet and harmonize: confidence (Mt 14,31), firm hope (Jas 1,6), fidelity to promises (Rom 3,3), trust and obedience (Rom 4, 20ff), intellectual acceptance of facts (Heb 11,6). Such a faith cannot be passive or inert but is accompanied by the "works" mentioned in Jas 2,21–24. This full faith, faith as total commitment, is the "faith that saves." (Rom 3,22.26; 4,24)[1]

Too often in the past Catholic writers have overstressed the purely intellectual element of faith (because this was the point under attack), and failed to emphasize the personal encounter and total commitment aspects. We must see faith as a response of our total personality, a

---

[1] A period between verse numbers indicates that the verses cited are successive but nonconsecutive.

response that reaches to daily living. For unless we accept Christ with a completeness that touches our everyday life, it will not be for *us* a saving message, but a sterile one.

FAITH IN CRISIS   We see around us one Christian who has "strong faith," another who is "losing his faith." In neither case are we thinking so much of the intellectual element, but rather of the total life of faith. It is this wholehearted acceptance of Christ which can fluctuate often and even undergo crises. Sometimes it is excessive love of self, or of something incompatible with Christ, which threatens our encounter or commitment; and here the resulting crisis is culpable.

But other crises are normal: for example, the reevaluation of reality and the "rethinking" of faith on an adult level are usually not accomplished without a crisis of faith. When the easy faith of the child is examined by the maturing mind as it is confronted by the outside world, questions arise. The child must be led to a reacceptance of Christ and his message on the adult level by seeing Christ somehow as the answer to his search for lasting truth, justice, and happiness. The Christian message cannot be forced upon him from outside. As long as it remains unwanted and foreign it will never be, for him, the good news of salvation. As long as a person is convinced that he has no need of God, faith will always seem an imposition to him.

The faith of the child is simple, unquestioning. Not so that of the adult. He must reassess reality and his goals on the adult level, and take stock of himself in terms of the whole world and even infinite realities. Only when he awakens (or reawakens) to his need for God and salvation does he really become "open" to a saving message, and capable of true adult response. Only then can he see Christ and his message as something welcome and not an imposition.

The influences at work in this maturing recommitment to Christ in faith are not easy to determine. But God's grace is always at work, and we need not ever lose our faith in order to "refind" it and bring it to a level worthy of our adult status. We ought never be surprised, however, at "doubts against the faith" involved in the necessary reappraisal of the personal encounter and commitment to which we are invited in the life of faith.

Restricted Notion of Faith

FAITH AS AN ASSENT OF THE INTELLECT   Once this full notion of faith is clearly in mind, we must speak of another legitimate and necessary view of faith: namely, as an assent of the intellect to truth revealed by God. This is seeing faith as knowledge. Protestants in general minimize this intellectual element, thinking of faith more in terms of trust and confidence (verging on hope, in the Catholic understanding of that virtue), or even the experience of God speaking within man's heart. The Council of Trent was counteracting this view when it defined faith as an act in which "by the inspiration and help of God's grace we believe that what he revealed is true, not because its intrinsic truth is seen with the natural light of reason, but because of the authority of God revealing, who can neither deceive nor be deceived." (D1789)

These truths of revelation, when proposed by the Church, are the dogmas of faith, the starting point of the further elaborations of theology. We would be betraying Truth itself were we to minimize the intellectual truths involved in the total message, in a false attempt to see faith as an attitude of life somehow devoid of intellectual basis and importance. Thus theologians tell us that faith is primarily an assent of the mind.

THE OBJECT OF FAITH   What is it we believe? Certainly we accept the individual truths and dogmas about Christ and God, but they are not the primary object of our faith. I am listening not merely to *something* (an isolated truth), but to *someone,* and I cannot really listen (in the best sense) to a person without its affecting me. Again we are back at the "I-Thou" relationship of persons. What is more, it is a *free* turning toward this person to accept what he says, and freedom involves the will and ultimately the whole personality.

Thus even on the intellectual level more is involved than appears at first sight. I believe God (*credo Deum*) as Truth itself which the intellect seeks; and I believe *in* God (*credo in Deum*) as Goodness itself, or that toward which I am impelled by my free will, as a goal to be attained.

Faith, then, does not stop at facts but at the person of God (Mk 11,22; 1 Thes 1,8; Heb 6,1) or of Christ. (Jn 11,25ff.45; 14,1) So, for example, faith in the resurrection does not stop at the words of the dogma but reaches on to the very mystery itself; nor does it stop at the mystery but only at the person of the resurrected Christ. (*S. Th.*, 2ª 2ᵃᵉ, 1,2 ad 2) The Christian tradition has always seen the essential object of faith in Heb 11,6: "For he who comes to God must believe that God exists and is a rewarder to those that seek him"; in other words, that God is the supernatural end of man. All the rest of revelation is but a clarification of this central truth, ways of "cutting up" the ultimate mystery of God to permit us to reflect and form more exact and precise ideas. This view of the ultimate object of faith shows the true enormity of heresy. For how willingly reject one "portion" of truth without rejecting Truth itself?

THE MOTIVE OF FAITH   The Christian does not believe the facts God reveals because he "sees" them, or because they seem reasonable, but simply because God—who is Truth—tells him about these mysteries.

Nor is it a question of believing "because the Church says it," but rather because God, whose message is preserved and presented by the Church, says it. Once again, it is important not to see the Church as a barrier; its infallibility simply guarantees that what it puts us in touch with is the pure message, the Word of God. So, for example, if my brother tells me that "mother says this," as long as I know he is reporting accurately, I believe it because my mother says it, not because my brother says it. The same thing can be said of believing God's revelation through the Church.

Before leaving the notion of faith, we should note that there is a stunted form of faith that can go on existing even when the believer is in the state of mortal sin, a faith without love or conformity of one's life and person to Christ and his message. Such is called "unformed faith," that is, not molded and perfected by love. Assent of this kind to revelation still merits the term faith (D838), but we ought not to suppose that we have the full notion in this imperfect manifestation; it is *19* rather something of a caricature.

THEOLOGY, THE EXPOSITION
AND UNDERSTANDING OF THE MESSAGE

Faith and Reason

Only now are we in a position to appreciate the place of theology in the Church, for it fits naturally into the picture of the message of salvation. Simply speaking it is nothing but the effort to find out exactly what the message is, and then to understand it better. Granted the fact that God has spoken to us in his Son, Jesus Christ, and the fact of man's natural drive to understand more and more perfectly the things that interest him, theology is not only legitimate but entirely natural. It must not be looked upon as an artificial pastime divorced from reality and inimical to true science.

Theology is not new to the Church. No sooner had men received the message of salvation than they began to use human reason to arrange, defend, and explore its content. The sacred writers themselves, though guided and protected by inspiration, were theologians too. St. Paul's brilliant mind is at work as he ponders the original message, and his teaching on original sin and the Church as the body of Christ are examples of deep insights he had into the mystery of Christ. The first chapter of St. John's gospel is another piece of profound theology. Still, in these cases we must remember that the theology or deeper awareness of the message on the part of the apostolic writers is for us part of revelation.

Nor did it take early Christianity long to apply the human mind to revelation. St. Irenaeus, bishop of Lyons (d. 202) so successfully defended Christian teaching against the heretics that he has been called the first theologian. Clement of Alexandria (d. 215) and his successor, Origen (d. 253?), organized the first great school of theology at Alexandria. There was much profound theology evident in the discussions of the early Church councils. St. Augustine (d. 430) contributed mightily to the understanding of grace, and Pope St. Leo I (d. 461) to the relationship of the divine and human natures in Christ. The middle ages brought the great systematizations of theology in the works of Peter Lombard, St. Bonaventure, and especially in the *Summa Theologiae* of

St. Thomas Aquinas (d. 1274). This trend has continued to our own day. It is not our intention to give a history of theology, but simply to point out that the application of reason to the realm of faith, far from being a recent innovation, stretches back to the beginnings of Christianity.

The I Vatican Council had to defend faith against the excessive claims of the rationalists who thought that reason would eventually do away with all mystery; but it also had to defend human reason against the traditionalists who thought it could play no worthwhile role in religion. The Council is merely restating long accepted views in holding that man can have two kinds of knowledge: one through faith, another through reason; that reason can play a vital part in the study of supernatural truth; that though faith is above reason, there can never be any real disagreement between them because it is the same God who reveals mysteries and infuses faith, and who has put the light of reason into the human soul. Further, they help each other: faith by guiding and correcting reason; reason by demonstrating the foundations of faith, defending it, and helping to understand it (D1795-1800). We may never consider theology the province of faith *or* reason, as if in a consideration of revealed truth they could be mutually exclusive, but of faith-enlightened reason.

Notion of Theology

Theology (from "*Theos*," God, and "*logos*," study) is defined as the science or discipline which, by the use of human reason guided by faith, treats of God and creatures insofar as they are related to God. In the simple words of St. Anselm, theology is "faith seeking understanding."

Every discipline has to have a starting point. Philosophy begins from what are called "self-evident principles" such as causality, identity, noncontradiction, and so on. Most disciplines (whether science or art) start with facts or conclusions already established; thus music starts from principles guaranteed by mathematics. What is the starting point of theology? Revelation, or the divine message. Here is the sure knowledge upon which it builds.

Theology ought not to be denied the title of true science (in the older sense, i.e., not confined to physical phenomena, as the natural sciences) since it performs all the functions of a science, namely: demonstrating the existence of its starting point, the revealed truths; defending them against doubt or denial as truly revealed; explaining and illustrating these truths as much as possible; deducing further knowledge and applications from them; assembling them, together with further conclusions, into harmonious arrangement, as is done in tracts and textbooks of theology. All these procedures are clearly scientific in character; and the systematic arrangement of truth which results clearly deserves the name of science. (Cf. *S.Th.* 1,1,2.8.)

Object of Theology

Every science is concerned with a definite area of knowledge, e.g., anatomy with the body and psychology with the mind. Theology's area, or what is called its *material object,* is God and creatures. But since several sciences may treat the same general area (material object), we must talk of the point of view each is concerned with; thus sociology and history both concern mankind, but from different points of view. Each science, then, has a *formal object.* Theodicy is the study of God and creatures as related to God, but as knowable from reason alone; theology covers the same area (material object), but from a vastly different point of view (formal object), studying God in his intimate life, namely, as known to us by revelation and faith, and creatures as related to this God of revelation.

The Light of Theology

Every other science goes about its work by the use, or light, of reason alone. Theology brings in something else, the light of faith. Theology's "light," then, is that of reason under the guidance of faith. Faith is its guiding star, which, far from hindering reason's progress, allows it to begin from absolutely certain starting points, and channels its efforts along the right path. So again we can accurately describe theology as nothing else than the exercise of reason, guided by faith, trying to take account of the revealed message.

22   It is precisely because theology excels all other sciences, first by the sublimity and surety of its starting principles given us by God him-

self and second by the excellence of its guiding light, that theology is called a *supernatural* science and dares to claim the title of the queen of sciences.

Divisions of Theology

Christ's message of salvation is one whole; but since the study of it covers such a vast area theology is divided in various ways. According to different subject matter, we have: (1) dogmatic theology which studies the intellectual content of revelation, and (2) practical theology which studies the application of it. This application results in: (a) moral theology, the message in terms of right and wrong human action; (b) ascetical theology, regarding Christian perfection; (c) mystical theology, regarding the contemplative life; (d) pastoral theology, concerning the care and government of souls; and (e) canon law, on the laws of the Church.

The present series aims at one field: dogmatic theology, the attempt to understand the message as well as possible. Each of the twelve volumes examines a successive stage in the unfolding of the divine message and plan of salvation.

Dogmatic theology itself is divided, according to method, into positive and speculative theology. The former is the establishment of the principles of theology, namely, the existence of revelation itself, and exactly how the Church presents it to our belief. The latter is aimed at coming to some understanding of this message by the use of reason, not merely for the sake of satisfying intellectual curiosity, but in order to see more clearly what our response must be. The reader should have some notion of the problems involved in both positive and speculative theology, both of which will be very much a part of our study in these volumes, but often, perhaps, without specific attention being called to the division.

Positive Theology

Positive theology inquires into the *existence* of a doctrine; for example, has God revealed the divinity of Christ? If so, in what terms? Has the Church formulated this belief in dogmas? For unless we know

23

the exact content of the revealed message, there is little use going on to speculative theology, which is the attempt to understand it better. Positive theology is particularly concerned then with the *sources* of the message, especially the Bible, and the history of the message—particularly its expression in early writings, in liturgy, in controversies against heretics; and finally its definitive formulation by the teaching Church.

Surely the clearest source of the divine message is the *Bible,* so it is essential to understand a good deal about it. Pope Leo XIII said in the encyclical letter *Providentissimus Deus:* "Let sacred Scripture influence all theological knowledge, and become, so to speak, its soul." (*ASS,* 26[1893-1894] 269-292; par. 99) We know that the Bible is the inspired word of God. Yet it is his message given to us in human language. Inspiration does not mean dictation, and even though the Holy Spirit used the human author as his instrument—so that the author wrote what God wanted—he was still a *human* instrument with all the individual traits of natural ability, with their dependence on milieu, background, and education, to be found in any man. Moreover, in order that the divine realities might be grasped by man, God saw that they were expressed in human words, images, and concepts. Thus what we have is the divinely inspired message wrapped in human expression; none the less true for all that, but needing to be understood as God and the author meant it.

In order to decipher, as it were, the word of God from its human wrappings we have to understand how much is divine, how much human. The Church is the final norm of what is taught in the Bible, but it by no means ignores the human aids which science can afford in trying to arrive at the true meaning. Philology, archeology, knowledge of ancient languages, a better understanding of Oriental manners of thought and expression, appreciation of literary and historical forms, all have helped the biblical scholar greatly in separating the nucleus of the divine message from its human and exterior expression.

Moreover, knowledge of the gradual formulation of the Bible, and especially the New Testament writings, shows the wisdom of tracing many doctrines through their successively clearer stages in Scripture. This is the reason for treating the Old Testament teaching on death, for example, before that of the New Testament, and the synoptic gospels before the Acts of the Apostles. Often St. Paul or St. John will have

24

a fuller picture of some teaching, not because it was fabricated by them (as some non-Catholic scholars have claimed) but because their age or individual insight reflects the consciousness of the gradually maturing Church, able to express better its experience of Christ.

In all this, two things are of utmost importance. First, the exegete must never take texts in isolation, but in the context of their over-all place in the message of God. Second, and most important, he must work with the guidance of faith under the Church's authority, for no interpretation can be true which conflicts with the living tradition of the Church. This is so not because the Church claims to judge the word of God, but precisely because the Church is the prior and living expression of God's continuing word. Hence the wise and absolutely necessary admonition that Scripture must be read *in* and *by* the Church.

Another area of positive theology is the study of early Christian writers, called globally the Fathers of the Church (of these, some but not all have this designation in a restricted sense). The Fathers are the witnesses to tradition, that is, to the message as it was continued, preached, and believed by the Church. From their writings as observant and faithful members of the Church, we can get a good picture of the divine message as it was being expressed and lived in a particular age. Closely allied with this is a study of worship and liturgies, where tradition again shows up dramatically. But in all of this, individual testimony is not so important as the consensus.

Finally comes the study of the doctrine in the official teaching body of the Church (the *magisterium*). From early times the Church, often under the pressure of threatening heresy, has found it necessary or advisable to concretize the message of Christ into dogmas. Many of these were the products of the ecumenical councils. To understand the import of the teaching, the theologian must know the background of the question, the personalities, and the terminology involved.

Such definitive and infallible judgments about revelation can be rendered by an ecumenical council in union with the pope, or by the pope alone; these constitute the solemn magisterium. Or again, a doctrine can be obligatory if held as revealed by the unanimity of bishops scattered throughout the world in union with the pope: what is known as the universal and ordinary magisterium. All revealed truth so given to us must be accepted by divine faith on the authority of God. (D1792)

25

Only matters of revelation can ever be defined as dogmas. However there are certain truths so connected with revelation that to deny them would endanger the very foundations of our faith; these are the secondary objects of infallibility, such as dogmatic facts (for example, that the Council of Nicea was truly ecumenical), and the canonization of saints (i.e., that they are truly in heaven). These truths are accepted on the authority of the infallible Church with what some theologians term "ecclesiastical," or mediately divine, faith.

Many teachings of the Church and theologians do not fall into these restricted categories. Hence are found several lesser "notes" or designations: certain teaching, common or less common opinion, probable and more probable opinion.

Thus by positive theology we arrive at a knowledge of the existence and particular status of the various truths of Catholic faith.

Speculative Theology

Speculation begins where positive theology leaves off; that is, given the precise formulations of the message of salvation, the human mind is impelled by a perfectly natural and legitimate desire to understand them better. If the human mind instinctively craves to delve into all sorts of problems, all the more should it attempt to grasp as fully as possible the saving message of God. There have been those in the history of the Church who deplored the application of reason to the truths of faith, considering it dangerous and presumptuous to delve into the mysteries of God. The Church has had to oppose this error as well as its opposite: given a long enough time human reason can eliminate all mystery (rationalism), or that even if some mysteries could not be known without revelation (e.g., the Trinity), once they are known reason will eventually be able to demonstrate them (semi-rationalism).

After stating that human reason has its limits and could never arrive at a knowledge of the strictly supernatural mysteries (Trinity, incarnation, eucharist, etc.) without revelation, the I Vatican Council goes on:

> It is nevertheless true that if human reason, with faith as its guiding light, inquires earnestly, devoutly, and circumspectly, it does reach, by God's generosity, some understanding of mysteries, and that

a most profitable one. It achieves this by the similarity with truths which it knows naturally and also from the interrelationship of mysteries with one another and with the final end of man. Reason, however, never becomes capable of understanding them the way it does truths which are its own proper object. For divine mysteries of their very nature so excel the created intellect that even when they have been given in revelation and accepted by faith, that very faith still keeps them veiled in a sort of obscurity, as long as "we are exiled from the Lord" in this mortal life, "for we walk by faith and not by sight." (2 Cor 5,6f) (D1796)

MYSTERY   Revelation is mysterious because God is revealing himself, and he is the Infinite. If our own personality is mysterious, how much more God's. No matter how much he reveals himself, God cannot reduce himself to finite dimensions; similarly, finite minds can never grasp or encompass the infinite. "When you think you know what God is," says Augustine, "it is then that you do not know."

Mystery is an enigma, but it is not therefore unintelligible. It is incomprehensible in the sense of unfathomable, not in the sense of unreasonable. Mystery is not a wall, but rather an ocean. A wall turns us back, but an ocean opens up the possibility of unbounded adventure and excitement. Or again, mystery is not like the obscurity of twilight, but like the obscurity of dawn, an obscurity that grows brighter and brighter until finally, like the noonday sun, it becomes so dazzling we cannot look upon it with the naked eye. (Cf. B. Murchland, *God Speaks*, pp. 28-30.)

ANALOGY   The Church teaches that we get a better understanding of the mysteries of God through analogy. I can apply the word "good" to a piece of steak and to a saint, or "life" to a tree, dog, man, and God. But we all realize that there are not only similarities but differences here. Analogy is the application of the same notion to two different things in ways which are partly the same, partly different. Thus while God and we both live, and the concept conveys real meaning, we must realize that life in God is very different from life in us, and that we are still far from understanding life in God by understanding what life means in us.

However, analogous knowledge is true, even though imperfect,

27

knowledge. God has chosen to reveal himself to us in our terms; he has spoken to us through the prophets and Jesus Christ his Son in human concepts, images, and words (such as father, son, love, anger, jealousy). But in applying these things to God, we must be careful to eliminate from them all the imperfections found in creatures. So, for example, in saying that God lives, we must not think of a life that begins, needs nourishment, involves change and finally death.

Even our knowledge through faith is analogous. "We see now through a mirror in an obscure manner," says St. Paul. (1 Cor 13,12) In the explorations of theology man's attempts to see more clearly are inadequate, halting, unsure. As long as he is aware of the limitations of this type of knowledge, however, he can advance.

Analogous ideas are like silhouettes. If we could not gaze upon the actual world itself, but had to arrive at an understanding of it by means of shadows cast by real objects and the relationship of these shadows, there are many facts of the real world that would remain unknown to us. Anything that failed to cause a change in the shape and size of the shadows would completely escape us. Still, these shadows do have some likeness to the bodies they represent. Think of the shadow cast by a tall man leading his small daughter by the hand, for example. Even from shadows, we can glimpse at least some knowledge, however imperfect, of the bodies themselves. (Gutberlet, *Lehrbuch der Apologetik,* II, 2nd ed., p. 18)

Some analogy is mere metaphor; to sing of God as the "rock of ages" is not to say that "rockness" is in God, but that the same quality of unchangeableness and stability is there. The same applies in calling Christ "The Lamb of God." This is analogy of improper proportion. But more important is analogy of being, or of proper proportion; thus, for example, the very essence of fatherhood is found in God in an infinite way and in us in a finite way. Because it is analogical, such a concept will never exhaust the content of revelation, but because it is proportionate, it will give an exact and unequivocal "something" of the reality expressed. In this way we can come to some real knowledge, for example, of what Christ as "the only begotten Son of God" means.

All knowledge of God is analogous. Yet certain non-Catholic theologians, particularly Karl Barth, think analogy blasphemous, reducing the transcendent God to the human level. However, they misunderstand analogy. For on the one hand it is only by analogy that we escape this very fault, and on the other that we are still able to have some true knowledge of God—and so avoid the agnosticism with which Barth is threatened. The validity of using analogy rests precisely on the fact that God first used it in communicating with us.

Analogy of faith is the second means that proves extremely fruitful in theology. It refers to the necessary procedure of always seeing one truth about God in relation to the total message and plan of salvation. No truth can be taken in isolation, no doctrine can be legitimate which conflicts with the rest of revelation. Thus for example no matter how deep our love for Mary, we can explain her role of advocate (*mediatrix*) legitimately only if we keep in mind the uniqueness of Christ's redemption and mediation. Or no matter how vividly we wish to describe the Mass, we may not say that Christ dies again, since the Epistle to the Hebrews clearly states that he died once for all and can die no more.

It is impossible, then, to discuss a Christian truth in isolation without ultimately distorting it in some way. *This* was usually the fault of heretics, who so concentrated their attention upon one point that they unwittingly distorted others.

Always mindful of the necessity of analogy and analogy of faith, the speculative theologian applies human reason to the mysteries in God for the following purposes:

(a) to systematize our knowledge of God into meaningful divisions: the tracts,

(b) to establish the preambles of faith,

(c) to show that the truths of faith do not contradict true reason; e.g., that the notion of three persons in one divine nature is not opposed to reason,

(d) to bring out the fittingness of revealed facts, even though we cannot demonstrate them; e.g., all the reasons that make it most reasonable to conclude to the doctrine of the assumption,

(e) to reconcile as much as possible seemingly opposed truths; e.g., God's absolute causality and human freedom,

(f) to deduce conclusions and further truths from revealed dogmas; e.g., from Adam's headship of the human race and original sin to the effects of his sin upon us,

(g) to bring out as completely as possible the meaning and beauty of mysteries; e.g., the sacrifice of the Mass and its relation to the Last Supper and Calvary, concerning which hundreds of books have been written by theologians.

Selected Readings

Bouyer, Louis, *The Word, Church and Sacraments* (New York: Desclée, 1961), pp. 7-56.

Callahan, D., H. Oberman, and D. O'Hanlon, eds., *Christianity Divided* (New York: Sheed and Ward, 1961), pp. 7-29.

Chenu, M. D., *Is Theology a Science?* (New York: Hawthorn, 1959).

Guardini, Romano, *The Life of Faith* (Westminster, Md.: Newman, 1961).

Heaney, J., ed., *Faith, Reason and the Gospels* (Westminster, Md.: Newman, 1961).

Henry, A. M., ed., *Introduction to Theology* (Chicago: Fides, 1954).

Journet, Charles, "Scripture and the Evolution of Dogma," in *Dogma of the Immaculate Conception*, ed. E. D. O'Connor (Notre Dame, Ind.: University of Notre Dame Press, 1958), pp. 3-48.

Mackey, J. P., *The Modern Theology of Tradition* (New York: Herder and Herder, 1963).

Levie, Jean, *The Bible: Word of God in Words of Men* (New York: Kenedy, 1962).

Moran, C. G., *Scripture and Tradition* (New York: Herder and Herder, 1963).

Mouroux, Jean, *I Believe: The Personal Structure of Faith* (New York: Sheed and Ward, 1959).

Murchland, Bernard, *God Speaks* (Chicago: Fides, 1960), pp. 9-49.

Newman, John Henry, *An Essay on the Development of Christian Doctrine* (Garden City, N.Y.: Image Books, 1960).

Rondet, Henri, *Do Dogmas Change?* (New York: Hawthorn, 1961).

THE ONE GOD

THE WORKS OF GOD REVEAL HIS EXISTENCE

"The heavens declare the glory of God, and the firmament proclaims his handiwork." (Ps 18[19],2)

(Courtesy, Ansel Adams)

CHAPTER ONE

THE EXISTENCE OF GOD

All too often the theological presentation of the One God is nothing but philosophy with a few trimmings of Scripture. It treats the existence and nature of God according to the outline of theodicy. But theology should start from God's supernatural revelation of himself, not from facts of everyday experience. Experience can and should be used to help reason to see the harmony between faith and reason; but it should never be primary. To begin our theology of God from man's point of view would be foolish. It could warp our whole concept of the God of faith, obscuring (or at least leaving till the end) the *personal* aspect of God and hiding the warmth and life of this God who out of love for us has chosen to communicate with us and invite us to intimate dialogue with him.

The path of philosophy is the path of *man* toward God. But the fundamental claim of Christianity is that there exists another path, that of *God* to man. God was not content to let men grope toward him; he has taken the initiative in this dialogue. And this very fact is what distinguishes and gives so much sureness to Christianity, and to the religion of Israel before it.

Reason and experience both can lead us to the knowledge of something worthwhile. But how much more vital and satisfying it is to experience goodness than merely to know it. In supernatural revelation God lets man experience him, offering himself to us in a way far warmer and more personal than the sum of all reasoned knowledge of him.

Father Bouyer illustrates the tremendous difference by the example of Robinson Crusoe on his island. At first he thinks he is alone; then clues gradually accumulate which lead him to suspect the presence of someone else on the island. First he sees footprints, which could be those of an animal. Then comes real evidence of a human being, such as the still warm remains of a fire. Little by little, from accumulated clues and reflections, Robinson begins to form a rather clear idea of his still invisible companion. Then one fine day he sees this person coming to meet him. From that moment on everything is changed. Not only will the knowledge he may have acquired of the other be corrected, enriched, and completed; it will become a quite new kind of knowledge: personal knowledge. And this renewed knowledge will transform not only Robinson's idea, but his whole life, precisely because the other, a living person and no longer just an idea in his head, has entered it. (L. Bouyer, *Christian Initiation,* p. 39-40)

The Church tells us that the same thing has happened in the relationship of man to God. He is no longer someone whose existence has been revealed to us by a number of clues, nor even someone of whom we have acquired a fairly profound knowledge by reflecting on these clues; God is henceforth someone who has spoken to us, who has intervened in our lives. He has spoken to us in history and still speaks to us through the Church; and not only has he spoken and acted in our behalf, but finally come among us in the person of Christ to enlighten and also to transform us.

GOD'S PATH TO US: REVELATION

The history of man's search for God, whether under that precise name or not, is a story of confusion, half-truths, and error. Modern man feels the need for God more than ever before, it seems. Yet such is his confusion that he even wonders at times if the very God he seeks is not just a myth dreamed up as an answer to his anxiety and yearning.

In looking at the Bible, the history of God's dealings with men, we are struck by the unquestioning assurance which marks the believer's awareness of God. The men of the Bible are not worried about laying philosophical foundations before admitting God is real; they are not afraid that he is just a monstrous projection of man's subjective needs and yearnings. For them God is simply there, despite all incomprehensibility and complete "otherness."

Though aware that reason can arrive at God (as we shall see), their assurance does not spring from this. Nor are they disturbed by seeing paganism or ignorance of God all around. They look upon such failure to see God as more a moral fault than anything else, that is, due to man's foolish heart. (Rom 1,21)

Why this calm assurance, then? Because of the simple fact that God has *revealed* himself. By word and action he has made his existence quite evident. He talks familiarly with Adam (Gn 2–3); Henoch walks with him (Gn 5,22ff); God chooses the Hebrews as *his* people and enters into an agreement with them (Gn 17,1–7), intervenes to free them from slavery in Egypt and later from exile, and speaks repeatedly to them through his prophets. These are but a few examples. In short, through word and action God is constantly with them. Living faith sees him everywhere at work.

For the men of the New Testament, the evidence is even more convincing. Their God is certainly the God of Abraham, Isaac, and Jacob, that is, the God of the Old Testament; but their knowledge of God is not derived merely from his self-disclosure in the past history of

37

their people; they experience the living reality of God in his *new* activity, for God reveals himself anew to them.

God has spoken to them in his own Son *now* (that is, in this new and definitive age of God's dealings with man, Heb 1,2), has now made known his saving grace (Tit 2,11; 3,4; 2 Tim 1,10) in the Son of God through whom they must come to faith in God. (1 Pet 1,21) The Son has declared God to them, whom no one has seen. (Jn 1,18) They have seen the Son of God with their own eyes, have heard him, and touched him with their hands. (1 Jn 1,1) Even before they are fully aware that Christ is God, they know God is coming to them in Jesus. All the more so afterward. To accept Christ fully is to come to know God. From this result the numerous expressions in which Christ and God are associated; for example, eternal life is the knowledge of the only true God and of him whom God has sent. (Jn 17,3) This is so true that the Jews who do not acknowledge Christ, the Son, are held not really to know God whose sons they are convinced they are even in virtue of the Old Covenant.

But the men of the New Testament are witnesses of the whole reality of Christ (Ac 2,22.32; 3,15; 10,39; 13,31) and have had the living, tangible experience of Christ, his miracles and resurrection. In Christ they have encountered God. They know him now by his personal, living, powerful action among them in Christ.

This is what is meant by saying that the men of the Bible do not worry about a carefully constructed philosophical conception of God. The primary thing for them is God's own concrete self-disclosure of himself. Their faith is a result of personal encounter with God in Christ. (See K. Rahner, "Theos in the New Testament," *Theological Investigations,* Vol. I, pp. 94-100.)

God knew it was *possible* for men to reach him along their own path. But he also knew the difficulties and errors that lay along this path. Very few men are good metaphysicians, whereas all men need to be saved. So God in his mercy and wisdom came to meet men in revelation. He thereby made it possible for everyone to know the whole saving truth easily, with absolute certitude, and with no trace of error. (D1786)

The history of peoples not yet favored by this supernatural revelation bears eloquent testimony to the wisdom of God's decision. God is knowable through the external things he has created and through conscience. But this kind of testimony (or "natural" revelation) is received by a humanity whose intellect and conscience are marred by the consequences of original sin; it finds difficulty in penetrating souls with its full integrity. The fact is that pagan religions are like rays of cosmic revelation refracted through a humanity spoiled by sin and not yet enlightened by positive revelation.[1]

MAN'S PATH TO GOD: CREATED THINGS[2]

Is human reason capable of arriving at the existence of God by its own efforts? This is a problem that has fascinated and torn philosophers from the beginning of the recorded history of that study. Does there exist a Being who is sovereign, eternal, infinite, unchangeable, all-knowing, almighty, the Creator of everything outside himself? If so, it is supremely important to know it; for in the attainment of him somehow will consist our final happiness.

For those who have been assured of God's existence through supernatural revelation, the problem is less urgent. Even if the believer could not know God otherwise, his belief would not be less solid. But what of the greater part of mankind which has not had this blessing? The destiny of all men is union with God; but how strive for something unless it is knowable? How could God hold responsible those who have not heard his revealed message, or who have not known Christ?

Nor should the believer be less interested. For he has to give an account of his faith to the best of his ability and to illustrate the perfect

---

[1] Cosmic revelation, of which the pagan religions are defective signs, is imperfect and incomplete revelation. It represents a past phase in the history of revelation; religions founded upon it alone are outmoded survivals of a past period in the history of salvation. To remain there deliberately would be wrong. It is in this sense that the religions or ethical systems of Buddha, Zoroaster, and Confucius are partially true, yet unacceptable. They can be seen as forerunners of Christ. But the function of a forerunner is to withdraw when he whom he is sent to introduce makes his appearance. (J. Daniélou, *God and the Ways of Knowing*, pp. 21f)

[2] Some apology is due for the comparative length of this section. If a college course in philosophy (theodicy) could be presumed, this would be unnecessary. But since for many students the only discussion of the rational proofs for the existence of God will be left to the theology course, it has been decided to include it here at somewhat greater length than would otherwise be the case. Even here, however, we shall try to keep the theological perspective.

harmony between faith and reason wherever possible. Thus it is important, especially in these days of science and doubt, for the adult Christian to be able to support his faith and have some grasp of reason's ability.

Many people today do not admit that human reason can arrive at the knowledge of God with any surety. The *agnostic* simply asserts that it is impossible to say anything about God, that a transcendent being is beyond our sphere of knowledge. The *skeptic* has, rather, a positive doubt about God's existence. The *atheist* denies God. We are not referring to the man who really admits God's existence, but in his everyday life acts as if God did not exist: this is the practical atheist. The true atheist is the man who has come to the absolute conclusion that God does not exist (or even *cannot* exist, as some would say). Such atheism is exemplified in communism and in the existentialism of Sartre.

The evidence from Scripture, from the constant teaching of the Church, and from sound philosophy clearly establishes the ability of the human mind to arrive at a knowledge of God's existence and of his essential attributes by its own power, starting from created things.

The Testimony of Scripture

"The heavens tell the glory of God, and the firmament proclaims the work of his hands" (Ps 18[19]2), chants the Psalmist. Yet we should not be too easily misled into thinking that the Hebrews saw God as the cause of all things in the sense that he made everything out of nothing. Actually the notion of creation came to them only very late in their history as a people. God revealed his identity to them at a time when it was inconceivable to them that there were no deities. He became known to them particularly by his power in delivering them from Egypt. Only later did they rise to a clear idea of his creative power. Thus they themselves did not have to reason to the existence of Yahweh.

In fact the Old Testament is not much concerned with our precise problem; Yahweh's existence is much too evident by his continual action on Israel's behalf: so much so, that the Israelites who "do not know God" do not really deny his existence, but rather question his influence over events (Is 46,6–11), or his knowledge (Ps 72[73]11), or his ability to judge clearly. (Jb 22,13f) The "fool" who says in his heart there is no God (Ps 13[14]1), along with the impious men who "deny" God (Jer 5,12), are practical atheists rather than real ones.

For the men of the Old Testament, even the pagans are not real atheists. They only fail to recognize the true nature of divinity, trying to find it in idols or the forces of nature. Pagans are regarded as those who have gone astray and in whom the notion of the true God has been obscured and degraded.

Only in the Book of Wisdom, probably the latest writing of the Old Testament and dating from the first century B.C., does the Old Testament take up explicitly the natural knowledge of God by the pagans. The author is bringing pagan idolatry to trial (chs. 13–15), and showing how illogical and culpable it is. After castigating Egyptian worship of animals, the worst of all turning from God (12,24), he is about to go back to his attack upon man-made idols. But before doing so he singles out another error, one more learned and less perverse than the other two types, namely, the divinization of the elements or of the great forces of nature. (13, 1–9)

The "pagans" mentioned here are philosophers and astrologers, men who think about the universe and who should be wise. They have a sense of the mystery of things; they attempt an explanation of the total universe, looking for God after a fashion. But they stop too soon, and do not push their investigations to the supreme explanation. Trapped by creatures, seduced by their beauty or power, they divinize them (v. 2): fire and wind (different conceptions of the Stoics' "pneuma" endowed with intelligence, and the principle of immanent divine energy in the universe), or the stars (seen as heavenly gods of great beauty), or the powerful sea (the Greeks had long ago divinized it), the sun and moon, and so on.

The pagans are reproached for not following the indications of nature herself. (v. 1) Nature should have led them to recognize the existence of a transcendent God, creator of the universe; but they do not read the evidence. They are blameable and responsible for their mistake. Right from the start they are called "vain," a biblical word with Greek overtones of "stupid," "absurd." Still, v. 6 calls them less culpable than those who worship man-made idols, for the latter worship lifeless things (v. 10); at least nature is living and serves to elevate the soul. The former are truly looking for a principle of things (v. 6); but they stop short, for nature is lovely (v. 7) to the point of giving the impression of divinity.

The text in Wisdom, then, insists that reason, starting from created things, the spectacle of nature (vv. 1.5), should lead to this natural knowledge of God's existence. The author implies that the step is relatively easy, if not spontaneous. Pagans who have failed to take the step are culpable. But note, he does not apply it to particular cases. In fact he seems to apply it directly only to a special category of pagans: the learned men of whom we have a right to expect a better use of the intellect.

We have seen the New Testament attitude toward knowledge of God: that he has revealed himself anew in Christ. Still, St. Paul in his Epistle to the Romans (1,18–23), clearly confirms man's ability to know God even without revelation. To make the Romans see the grandeur of the salvation wrought by Christ for all men, Paul first stresses the depths of their degradation. Verses 18–23 are the beginning of a picture he paints of the moral wretchedness of paganism. The prime source of this degradation of the pagan world lies in religious error. (v. 18) It could have known God through reason, but did not.

God, he says, has manifested to us truths that can be known about him (v. 19)—meaning not everything about himself, but what can be known through creation. Paul seems to underline three (v. 20): omnipotence in creating; eternity in prior existence; and transcendence (complete "otherness") in infinitely surpassing creation. All this God has manifested through the created world that is like an open book in which we can read the invisible perfections of God.

There seems to be a real resemblance between the passage of Romans and that of Wisdom, each teaching that by reflection on the marvels of creation man can come to the conclusion of the existence of a supreme Being who is the source of all. Whether Paul made use of the prior text is much disputed. But what is certain is that the theme of knowledge of God from the works of creation is common to late Judaism: for example, it is found in the Testament of the Twelve Patriarchs, the Fourth Book of Ezra, and the Syriac Apocalypse of Baruch. It seems to be a sort of apologetical approach familiar to the Jews coming into contact with the Gentiles. We see Paul using it twice: in Acts 14,15–17 at Lystra, and in Acts 17,24–27 at Athens.

But now to speak of Paul's originality in Romans. Everywhere else the pagans are reproached for *not* having known God. But Paul dares to say (1,21) "Men *have* known God, but have not glorified him." This is all the more startling because elsewhere he calls the gentiles people who live in ignorance of the true God. (1 Thes 4,5; 2 Thes 1,8; Gal 4,8) What is he getting at here? Certainly his opinion has not changed in the short space of time between these letters.

The Book of Wisdom stresses man's initiative in rising from created things to God by a process of reason. But Paul has a more biblically minded notion (than this one derived from the Greek philosophers), namely, that it is God himself who is taking the initiative, "manifesting himself to them through creation." (v. 19) That is, in creating the world God has in some manner obliged it to transmit to man a message, and if he has given men intellects, it is precisely so that they may be able to decipher the message. If man but remained "open," the message would come through.

A great change took place in man's way of acting, however. The universe did not stop speaking to him of God, but men "became vain in their reasonings, and their senseless minds have been darkened." (v. 21) The message of creation was obscured by pride, and men exchanged the glory of the incorruptible God for idols. Paul is describing the original fall of humanity and its passage from monotheism to polytheism and idolatry. Such disorders did not always exist, he says. In the beginning men knew God, that is, the message that creation delivered came through to them. But then pride made them lose the true sense of it, blinded them, rendered them incapable of understanding the language of creation. He calls all pagans guilty who do not know God, because he is thinking primarily of the origins of paganism, and the reason for its continued ignorance of God. Is this not the sense of v. 18, which speaks of the wickedness of men "which holds back the truth of God," as if the message were still ready to pour in on them if moral faults were not holding it back?

We should not be too quick to apply universally the picture of moral decay which Paul paints here. He is thinking of the Graeco-Roman civilization in full decay around him. It would be unjust to apply it to all pagans of all times. There has been much moral grandeur among them at times. We have only to think of Aristotle, Socrates, certain groups in China or India, the strong strains of monotheism in Africa and the Pacific Islands. Even Paul nuances his statements later (2,12–16) when he speaks of Gentiles who are saved by acting according to their consciences. That is, besides the testimony of God delivered by the exterior world, God has imprinted a certain knowledge of his moral law (and so of himself) upon the hearts of all men. Fidelity to this testimony can lead to the salvation of the pagan, a fidelity which involves, once more, not just man's intellect but his whole personality. (A. Feuillet, "La Connaissance naturelle de Dieu par les hommes, d'après Romains 1,18–23," *Lumière et Vie*, n. 14[June, 1954], 63–80)

In short, Wisdom seems to put the accent upon man's intellect alone in coming to the natural knowledge of God. St. Paul brings in another important element (which we shall see as very important in grasping the rational proofs), namely, moral integrity. It is within the people of God that the human intellect has arrived at the fullness and the integrity of its normal exercise. In other words, intellectual effort is not independent of man's total being and way of life. The understanding and knowledge of God are inseparable from holiness. It is in freeing man from pride, injustice, and evil that God has enabled man to know him. While such moral "openness" to God is occasionally found among the pagans, it is a rarity. Man best rediscovers his real freedom, wisdom, and understanding, and so his natural openness to God, by rediscovering God in Christ (as in the religion of Israel before him).

As we shall see in considering the rational arguments, nothing will convince a person who does not wish to be convinced. St. John tells us that the intellect can *prefer* the darkness to the light. (Jn 1,5) It can choose to be darkened; as Paul says, "They have held truth prisoner in injustice, they have misled themselves in the vanity of their own reasoning, and their hearts have been darkened in misunderstanding." (Rom 1,18.21) (See C. Tresmontant, "Biblical Metaphysics," *Cross Currents*, 10 [Summer, 1960], 233–234.)

The Testimony of the Church

Starting from the biblical data, the Fathers of the Church in their
44 controversies with the pagans, Manicheans, and Gnostics, often teach clearly that the knowledge of God arises in man naturally—and almost

spontaneously—from consideration of created things. Theophilus of Antioch is a good example.

> God has called everything into existence from nothing, so that
> his greatness might be known and understood through his works.
> Just as the soul of man is not seen, as it is invisible, but is known
> through the movement of the body, so God cannot be seen with
> human eyes; but he is observed and known through providence and
> his works. Just as one, at the sight of a well-equipped ship which
> sweeps over the sea and steers towards a harbor, becomes aware that
> there is a helmsman on her who directs her, so also one must be
> aware that God is the director of everything, even though he is not
> seen with bodily eyes. . . . *To Autolycus,* 1,4–5)

Some even spoke as if this knowledge of God were innate; they
used terms such as "not learned," "automatically learned," "implanted."
But in context they seem to mean that such knowledge is easily had.
St. Thomas Aquinas says that the knowledge of God is innate in us
only insofar as we can easily know the existence of God by means of
principles which are innate in us. All the scholastic theologians have
steadfastly upheld the ability of human reason to arrive at a knowledge
of the existence of God.

However, scholasticism fell into disrepute, and scientific minds
became imbued successively with the idealism of Descartes, the rationalism of Kant, and the positivism of Hume and Comte. All these involved
an exaggerated emphasis on human reason to the detriment of faith and
led ultimately either to the denial of God or the claim that given enough
time human reason could come to understand even the great mysteries
of God.

Disillusioned with the extravagant claims of the rationalists who
exalted human reason, the traditionalists, so called, of the nineteenth
century erred at the other extreme by underestimating the ability of individual reason to arrive at truth. Truth and certainty, they said, are only
possible because of a primitive revelation made to Adam, revelation
which has been preserved and passed on to us. But since individuals
can be mistaken about it, some social authority is needed; this is the
Catholic Church. One should not try to pursue the truths of religion
by human reason, but simply accept what the Church says. This extreme, as much as its opposite, the Church was quick to oppose.

45

The I Vatican Council (1869-1870) was much concerned about the reconciliation of faith and reason. In upholding the true worth and dignity of human reason it said the following:

> God, the origin and end of all things, can be known with certainty by the natural light of human reason from the things he created, "for since the creation of the world his invisible attributes are clearly seen, being understood through the things that are made." (Rom. 1,20) (D1785)

> If anyone says that the one true God, our Creator and Lord, cannot be certainly known from created things by the natural light of reason, let him be condemned. (D1806)

Thus it is *of faith* that human reason alone, apart from supernatural revelation, can know God with certitude by way of created things.

The Council is speaking only of the *possibility* of knowing God by reason. It does not say whether and how often this possibility is realized, nor what part supernatural grace plays, nor what is the relative importance of intellectual, volitional, and moral factors, nor whether language, education, and training of the religious sense are necessary factors.

Early in this century the heresy of modernism came into prominence. It did not deny that God can be known with certainty. However, for the modernist, there is no way to demonstrate this certainty: it simply arises from within, from the principle of vital immanence; that is, from the need for God within the human soul. You can never demonstrate the existence of God to another, says the modernist; the most you can do is lead him to experience the same need.

In his condemnation of modernism, Pope Pius X extended the "able to be known with certainty" of the Vatican Council to "able to be demonstrated." (D2145) This clarification is not of faith, but is to be held as certain teaching of the Church. We should note that the Church is not denying that some people may be subjectively convinced of God's existence because of an interior, "felt" need. It simply asserts that this is not the only way, and that objective demonstration is possible.

The Testimony of Reason

46   Scripture and the Church assure us that the existence of God can be demonstrated by human reason starting from created things. There

is no one way to present the arguments, nor any strict enumeration of them. However, it seems best to divide our discussion as follows: the possibility of experiencing or intuiting (i.e., knowing directly, apart from the avenues of sense) God's existence; the arguments based on the moral consciousness of man; the "classical" or metaphysical arguments; and finally some concluding remarks which apply to man's whole attempt to apprehend God by reason.

THE POSSIBILITY OF DIRECT CONTACT, IMMEDIATE EXPERIENCE, OR INTUITION   If a friend is standing beside you, talking to you, helping you, there is no need to prove he exists before welcoming him. Were God's relationship to us like this, we would need no proofs. And in fact the mystics—both Christian and non-Christian—have often claimed to have a kind of direct and immediate intuition of God. God is simply present to them. So varied is the background, religion, and culture of these people, and so striking their testimony, that it is impossible merely to discount their claims. (See L. Bouyer, *Christian Initiation,* pp. 32-36.) But this is a supernatural phenomenon; it is God's work, unusual and not communicable to others. The best we can do is take the mystic's word for it. We cannot have it by our own efforts. Such testimony is not, then, a strict proof.

Others, such as the Catholic existentialist thinker Gabriel Marcel, hold to a *natural* experience of God which is available to anyone who makes the effort. Marcel is of the opinion that rational proofs only convince those who already believe. What is necessary for this initial belief is a total commitment of self to the person of God—a sort of prior gift of self. To such generosity God responds, presenting himself not as an abstract idea but as a concrete person: as the "absolute Thou." There is much of this, too, in Maurice Blondel (d. 1949), who maintains that it is in our very act of loving God that we become conscious of him within us. We do not have to search outside reality for God; he is immanent within reality and especially within us. In this way, we begin to experience the God "in whom we live, and move, and have our being." (Ac 17,28) These ideas, noble as they are, are uncomfortably close to fideism, the position that God is knowable by faith only and not by reason. It is ultimately irrational to make a blind commitment to something which one is not sure as yet even exists.   47

St. Augustine and modern writers such as de Lubac speak more tellingly of being able to perceive obscurely the presence of God within us, even before any commitment of self. Such experience is natural in the sense that it demands simply an effort of reflection, or "openness," which can be made by anyone. Augustine relates how he searched in a "deformed" way for God everywhere, when all the time he needed only to have looked within himself. "You were within me, and I without." (*Confessions*, 10,27,38)

Even St. Thomas does not hesitate to speak of a certain confused knowledge of God which almost all men have, prior to any formal reasoning about him. (*S.C.G.* 3,38) This is borne out by the fact that the vast majority of men of all times have believed in God—a fact solidly established from the study of anthropology, history, and sociology. Many even maintain that the atheist recognizes God by a different name, for example, Future Humanity. In any case, the generality of this belief presents a solid presumption of its truth. As a matter of fact, it would seem that the "classical" proofs from causality are but the explicit, logical formulation of a basic and unpremeditated causal inference that takes place in all of us.[3] Still, such experience of men is not real scientific proof, however persuasive it may be for some.

THE ARGUMENTS BASED ON THE MORAL CONSCIOUSNESS OF MAN
From the psychological point of view this is by far the most common way of coming to God. Very few come by way of sheer intellectual conviction; in large measure they come through "the pressures of the heart."

---

[3] The distinction between explicit and implicit reasoning comes in here. People are often embarrassed if asked to give the motives for their action; and yet they *know* they have objectively valid reasons, even if not expressible in syllogisms. How many times we draw a conclusion, but in an implicit manner, from a number of facts. We are quite sure of our judgment, too, even though we have not waited for a formal, explicit process of deduction. It is a question of "good sense," or "good judgment." In more extraordinary cases we speak of "intuitions of genius." But it is always the intellect at work. This special faculty of judging concrete situations rapidly is what Cardinal Newman called the *illative sense*. By it a person is capable of judging even complex cases rapidly, or seeing intellectually the point of convergence of many probabilities. These probable arguments converge upon one point with so much force that it would be unreasonable not to see this point or conclusion as something certain. Thus, for example, from all sorts of little indications the shepherd or sailor is able to have certitude about tomorrow's weather. (See J. H. Newman, *Grammar of Assent* [Garden City, N.Y.: Image Books, 1955], pp. 260ff.)

There is much truth in Pascal's statement: "It is the heart that feels God, and not the reason." Still, these demands of the heart, or of the moral life and consciousness, are not irrational. They include a process of reasoning (however implicit in most cases) which leads to the acceptance of God.

The Meaning of Life. Has life any meaning? Our moral consciousness answers with an emphatic Yes. To deny this (or to say it is just a matter of training and environment) is to leave conduct without importance, good and evil equal. Principles of justice, truth, goodness and so on must, then, be founded upon some absolute Truth, Goodness, Justice. Moral value seems to demand God.

Man's Desire for Happiness. This is often called the psychological argument, and thinkers from Augustine to the present have made effective use of it. It springs from an analysis of the human will: nothing can ultimately appease its unrest, fill up its insatiable yearning for happiness, but the possession of perfect, infinite, and unlosable goodness— which can be found only in God. Experience shows that every man seeks happiness; that is the goal of all his efforts. Yet all the promising things offered or actually acquired in this world sooner or later disappoint him. Sometimes they elude his pursuit. Having won them, he may lose them, or, if he does not lose them, he has the disillusioning experience of finding that they no longer satisfy. He is still hungry. Either our human nature has no meaning, which is unthinkable, or else there exists a good, a happiness, capable of attainment and for which we were made, that will perfectly satisfy the human heart. Nothing less seems capable of filling up the longing and emptiness we all carry within ourselves. This perfect, infinite good is God. Such is Augustine's theme of the "restless heart" (found often in his *Confessions*). Nothing is more touching and convincing than Augustine's search for God through the various finite goods in which men ceaselessly hope to find happiness.

The Argument from Conscience. Deeply and irradicably rooted in man is a sense of duty and moral obligation which controls his thought and conduct. There is a basic, unchanging, absolute, and universal rule to do good and avoid evil. Though men may differ about specific details, 49 all see a basic obligation. It is not reasonable to attribute this merely to the result of vague, general, cosmic forces. The absolute character of the moral obligation, the appeal it makes to our very highest and proudest faculty—our free will—lead us to discern, behind and above our conscience, someone greater than ourselves who speaks to us in the depths of our being, who is always there waiting for us. This "someone" is the infinite Lawgiver, God. The thread of this argument runs all through Cardinal Newman's brilliant *Oxford University Sermons* and his *Grammar of Assent*.

The Argument from Moral Sanction. This is intimately tied to the preceding one. A moral order demands the triumph of good over evil, demands the reward of virtue and the punishment of wrongdoing. The human heart itself cries out for such justice. Yet all too often retribution does not come about in this life, crime seems to pay, and virtue goes unnoticed or even despised. There would never be a sufficient reason for living virtuously, as conscience demands, unless there existed an ultimate Rewarder and Punisher who takes care of this in a future life.[4]

The effectiveness of this approach to God should not be discounted. It is a touching argument, especially for the good and the unfortunate. However, it is founded on the none too solid basis of moral sentiment, and seems to put the cart before the horse, that is, morality before metaphysics, when actually the moral life logically presupposes a metaphysical order and is founded on it.

We are not saying that all or any of the preceding arguments are absolutely convincing, objectively speaking. But they are the ones which affect us most deeply, and prevent us from thinking of the problem of God as unreal. They lead us to see that there is no real solution to the vital problem of duty and to the vital search for happiness except by

---

[4] Immanuel Kant (d. 1804) based his whole case for the existence of God upon this argument. He denied the possibility of metaphysics by denying that the laws of causality were applicable outside this world. But he sincerely wanted to preserve God, and thought to do so not by pure reason, but by the practical reason. He considered the only and sufficient proof for God that based on the needs of moral life and conscience. His argument in brief: In man's heart lies the need and demand for justice. But it is not satisfied in this world, where too often the just man is unhappy and the wicked one prospers. Thus there must be another life (postulate of immortality) and a God who brings about justice, rewarding the just and punishing the evil, according to their merits (postulate of divinity).

belief in a personal God who is infinite knowledge, love, goodness, and rewarder.

Without wishing to play down the objective value of the "classic" arguments to be mentioned next, it is good for us to remember that men are human beings of flesh and blood, with heart, emotions, and desires as well as intellect. Separated from their human, concrete, existential substructure, the classical arguments are, in Pascal's words, "so metaphysical and involved that they are not very striking." In themselves they are perfectly logical and rigorous; but their psychological effect can be weak, precisely because man is not pure reason. Unless he feels the "need" for God, his answer may well be, "So what?" Hence the foregoing arguments have tremendous conditioning value. They are a good and even necessary springboard to the classical ones.

THE METAPHYSICAL OR CLASSIC ARGUMENTS   These arguments proceed not from the realities within our consciousness but from the external world, and lead necessarily to God as ultimate explanation. Most of them go back to Aristotle and were later taken over by St. Thomas and subsequent Christian philosophers; hence the term "classic" arguments. Starting from observable facts in this world, these argue: (a) from motion to an unmoved mover; (b) from things caused to a first efficient cause of all; (c) from nonnecessary things to the necessary being; (d) from degrees of perfection or of being to the perfect being; and (e) from order of the world to a supreme orderer.

Such proofs all suppose a realist theory of knowledge; for if a person denies the objective value of experience and the ontological value of first principles,[5] nothing is left. But if they are accepted (and any valid philosophy does accept them), then this demonstration unfolds with perfect logic, fully satisfying at least to the abstract reason.

The Argument from Motion.   Things in the world move; this

---

[5] Meaning the objective validity of what are known as self-evident principles, upon which true philosophy must be based. These are, for example, the principle of noncontradiction: that a thing cannot be and not be at the same time and in the same way; and the principle of sufficient reason: that for everything that happens, there must be a sufficient reason to explain what takes place. Such principles are known and applied by *all* men in their everyday life, though without reflecting upon them.

is an incontestable fact of experience. But everything in movement must be moved by something else. (Why? Because it cannot be the cause of its own movement, since movement is a "becoming," a perfecting in some way. If a thing caused this in itself, it would be in potency and in act with respect to the same movement—which violates the principle of non-contradiction). But in looking for the cause of its movement we cannot stop at something which is itself moved, else we have not explained anything. And we cannot suppose an infinite series of movers, each intermediate and itself moved by another. There must, then, be a first Mover which is itself unmoved. This is God.

Two things must be noted. First, the term "movement" is taken in a metaphysical sense, not just as change from one place to another, but as any passage from potency (mere capacity) [6] to act (a perfection); for example, from nonexistence to existence, from capacity to speak to speaking; from capacity for growth to growth. Secondly, the proof does not attempt to go back from mover to mover, or cause to cause, in time (or on what might be called a horizontal level—for example, tracing a child back through its ancestors; for here you find only accidental movers or causes, which might very well explain the appearance of the effect, but not the reason for its here-and-now existence). What the discussion is about is the impossibility of going back in a series of essential causes (vertically, so to speak, from the total series "up" to an adequate explanation of the series), that is, causes whose action is here-and-now necessary for the effect to be produced.

The possibility of going back to infinity is absurd, not in the accidental order (at least philosophically), but precisely in the order of essential here-and-now causes of the movement in terms of reduction from potency to act. It is not a question, therefore, of counting back to a God, who, as it were, gave everything a push at the beginning of time, but of understanding that *at the present moment* none of these observed intermediate movers will work unless there be another type of mover working on them—namely, one who is outside the whole series, who moves without being himself moved. This is only possible if there

---

[6] What makes these proofs difficult for the average reader is the need for some understanding of what is meant by potency (inherent capacity of a thing for becoming something more, or more perfect, or being added to in some way), and act (the determining element which brings to perfection what is in potency).

exist a being which is unmoved mover precisely because he is *pure act,* above all becoming or being perfected. And this is God.

The Argument from Causality.   We observe in the world around us all sorts of causes and effects; for example, a hammer blow is the cause of the nail being driven into the wood. But finite causes cannot explain their own efficient causality. To cause itself to act does not lie within the power of the hammer; nor does it lie within the power of any finite thing to perfect itself by becoming what it was not (a movement from potency to act). Something outside it must be the cause; in other words, the moving hammer is truly the cause of one effect but is itself the effect of a simultaneous cause. And we cannot go on to infinity in a series of here-and-now subordinate causes. Suppose a chain is hanging on a wall; the cause of the lowest link's remaining where it is cannot be explained ultimately by mere reference to the links above—even if we could think of an infinite series of links. For without a first efficient cause which is itself uncaused, there is no explaining the intermediate causes or links. And such a first cause remains uncaused; it cannot be "actuated" simply because it perfectly *is.* And this is God.

The Argument from Contingency, or Nonnecessary Beings.   Everything around us is dependent and contingent; in other words, it is able not to be. Things are corruptible, they come and go. Nothing explains its own existence. Existence (its act of being) is not a necessary part of any thing's essence (its "whatness"); for example, we can think of a dog, or anything else in this world, without thinking of it as necessarily existing. If this is the case with all things, if it is possible for all things not to exist, then at some time in the past nothing would have existed.[7] But from nothing comes nothing; so today, nothing would exist —which obviously is not true. Hence the only conclusion is that there must exist a Necessary Being who is not dependent in any way upon another, simply because he exists from himself and not from another. This is God.

The Argument from Grades of Being or of Perfection.   Among

---

[7] That is, granted the world had existed long enough; for then all possibilities would have materialized—including the state where none of these nonnecessary things existed.

things there are grades of goodness, truth, nobility, love, perfection. The only reason we can speak of "more" or "less" concerning such qualities is because of their proximity to or remoteness from a maximum, an absolute. There would, in fact, be no reason for distinguishing degrees unless there were an Absolute, which is not only perfection itself, goodness itself, and so on, but even being itself—actually the ultimate of all perfection. And this is God.

The Argument from Order of the World, or from Final Causality. All things in the world work harmoniously toward their goals and best interests, the smallest plant life as well as the human body. The most intricate and precise perfection is found in such things. But only intelligent creatures can choose their own goals. Hence nonintelligent nature —and ultimately the universe itself—must be directed or ordered to its goal by a supreme orderer or intelligence which is its own end, precisely because it is its own infinite realization or perfection, because it is its own "to be." And this is God.

At this point it is well to understand that the five classic arguments can be (and often are) used in an ordinary, nonscientific way. For example, to show that God exists one can point to the wonderful complexity of the human eye and make a very appealing argument for the necessity of a supreme orderer, God, who is the cause of such well-planned results. Or, as varying degrees of warmth in things can lead us to the fire which is its cause, so the degrees of goodness and perfection lead us back to an ultimate goodness and perfection which is the cause of all the lesser degrees.

These are examples of the common sense application of causality. This is not rigorous demonstration, but it *satisfies* good sense. Most people will be satisfied: in fact, it may well be that deeper solutions will leave them confused and unmoved. Hence the justification of staying on the common sense level, even though the perfectionist may scoff.

It is well to note that more exacting demonstrations are possible, and should be used for those capable of following them. We really are not going beyond the level of common sense, however, when we simply accumulate scientific facts, however impressive these facts may be: examining minute chromosomes, citing the enormous distances between galaxies of stars, and so underlining the enormity of the perfection in the phenomena observed. All these can illustrate; but we are not at the heart of the classical proofs until we realize that the causality St. Thomas speaks about is not on the level of phenomena, but in another order entirely, namely the order of metaphysics. To understand this world of metaphysics one has to understand what is meant by such terms as "being," "act," "potency," and so on.

Probably the clearest argument from this strict point of view is the third one, which argues from the idea of nonnecessary beings to the existence of a necessary being. This proof presupposes at its starting point merely the acknowledgment of some thing as existing in this world: a man, dog, oak tree. Of any such thing we cannot say it simply *is*. Its type of existence is limited by its nature. It "is" only in the limited way in which a dog or tree can be. It need not exist; it could just as well not exist; even when it does exist for a limited time, it is in the restricted existence allowed by the essence or nature of a dog or tree. It does not explain itself, then. It does not have its existence from itself or, it does not have within itself the explanation of why it exists. It is what we call dependent: owing its existence (its act of being), to something else. The human mind will not be satisfied until it concludes to the existence of some Being who does not owe his existence to any other—and precisely because he does not *participate* in being, but *is* being itself. One does not have to say of him "He is, but only as a man," or "He is, but only in the way in which a dog can be"; but simply "He *is*." He is, and to the point of coinciding with his very act of being. This is God. (See H. Paissac, "Les Preuves de Dieu," *Lumière et Vie*, n. 14 [June, 1954], pp. 91 ff.)

Another thing that the mature student should realize is something of the difficulty of using these classic arguments in the modern world of science. The first four boil down to efficient causality, the fifth to final causality; unfortunately in a world that is antiphilosophically oriented there is much questioning of the validity of applying causality outside this world of phenomena, or even at all.

David Hume (d. 1776), the English philosopher, started a great trend of thought known today as positivism. According to this theory, what our senses tell us about the reasons for things has nothing to do with true causality, but merely with succession of events; for example, the death of a soldier merely *follows* his being shot; that is all we can be sure of; to conclude to strict cause and effect is unwarranted. Hume and the positivists deny all causality.

Immanuel Kant (d. 1804), on the other hand, sincerely attempting to save true science, insisted that we can reason to cause and effect from phenomena observed; but he thought that this principle could not be validly applied outside the world of phenomena. Hence the principle: causality *in* the world, but not *of* the world. Kant effectively denied the possibility of metaphysics. Much of the scientific world today is heavily influenced by Hume and Kant.

Perhaps because of such widespread (but illegitimate) denial of the basic possibility of applying causality outside the world of phenomena, even some Catholic writers today insist that (whatever the abstract possibility) we do not demonstrate God to the modern mind, and that these proofs only convince those who already believe. This is particularly the case with Christian existentialists, such as Gabriel Marcel, who insist on taking man in his whole concrete life and situation. They insist that man can move toward God only by a movement of his entire personality, never by abstract reasoning.

This much can be said in all certainty: no matter what type of argument for God's existence is used, no matter how valid it may be in itself, it can only be valid *for us* if we accept it on our part with honesty and moral uprightness of heart. Why? Because even after all the proofs we do not *see* God as we see water after combining oxygen and hydrogen; God remains a *necessary conclusion*. And as long as we do not *see* something, we can always find reasons to object. In other words, the proofs for God do not *make* us believe, as do proofs from experience. Thus as Marcel says, even the classical proofs are but "ways of approaching the ontological Mystery." Perhaps St. Thomas was fully aware of this when he called his arguments "viae," ways or directions.

Hence, although the Church teaches that demonstration of the existence of God is possible for the human mind, it says nothing of the frequency of men's coming to God this way. The problem of scientific demonstration to the modern mind is far from simple. Pius XII acknowledged this in the encyclical, *Humani Generis*, when he said that human reason can indeed demonstrate with certainty the existence of God, but can only do this safely and well when properly trained, that is, when imbued with sound philosophy. (D3020)

56

SOME CONCLUDING REMARKS   *First,* we must hold to the possibility of rigorous demonstration of God's existence even apart from revelation. *Second,* there is no way of knowing how often men are brought to God by this way alone. Since men do not seek intellectually what they do not want, they must be led to see and feel their need for God. Hence the value of arguments which start from "the pressures of the heart." Only when modern man sees God as not just *some thing,* but as a *person* who can complete him in some way, will he begin to have that "openness" of mind and heart that is indispensable to the search for God. Thus, the moral arguments should precede the metaphysical ones and not be put in as mere corollaries. *Third,* since the aim of these arguments is not ultimately scientific, but to convince individuals about God, there is no need to use the most objectively valid proof. It may well be that a less perfect proof will touch the "whole man" far more intimately than the closely reasoned proof from contingency. In order that a truth be recognized, it is often not enough that it be evident in itself, nor even that it be well presented, but that it be presented in terms to suit the listener. *Fourth,* the role of God's grace must not be overlooked by the theologian. It may well be that in actuality no man comes to admit God's existence who is not conditioned, influenced, and moved by the help of God's grace (we are not saying revelation) to experience the need and desire for him, and so come to that indispensable "openness" spoken of. What does being "open" or well-disposed mean? It means primarily humility, a lack of self-centeredness. Christ's only real anger was with proud people, those who were so introverted they could not look at the world and its evidence. For the humble, good man, the existence of God is easy to see. The subtle and proud logician can get himself into an inextricable mess; whatever leads to God becomes horribly complicated. Thus there is the paradox that the proofs for the existence of God can be both simple and complicated; the evidence is brilliantly clear or else profoundly obscure, depending on the moral dispositions of the subject. *Last,* the Catholic knows that such demonstration is possible; but he is not too shaken if he himself cannot follow the arguments. In fact, most believers do not feel the need to prove to themselves the existence of God. Should he wish to verify (and he should) the premises of his faith in order to avoid all fideism, the believer has God's revelation. God has revealed his existence through the whole history of his dealings with the Israelites and most of all through Christ and the Church. The cumulative impact of all this can be so great, for some at least, that there can be no doubt for them of God's existence.

It is precisely because the Christian believes and is "attuned" that when the time comes for rational investigation, he will nearly always be content (much to the disgust of the philosophical rigorist) with a few striking examples: the marvels of the human body or the delicacy and perfection of a snow crystal. Such wonders seem to lead to an almost immediate conclusion: God exists. The rigorist could easily point out inadequacies, but reasons which are more or less "felt" satisfy the believer on the level of common sense and ordinary life.

THE BIBLE: WORD OF GOD

"Just as from the heavens the rain and snow come down and do not return there till they have watered the earth, making it fertile and fruitful, giving seed to him who sows and bread to him who eats, so shall my word be that goes forth from my mouth." (Is 55,10f)

(*Codex Washingtoniensis* (W), fourth-fifth century. Greek uncials. Courtesy, Smithsonian Institution, Freer Gallery of Art, Washington, D.C.)

CHAPTER TWO

WHAT GOD IS

In getting to know what God is, it is more important to see how he has revealed his "whatness" than how philosophers deduce it. True, theodicy can tell us the essential facts about God and how his attributes flow with inexorable logic from his essence. But this is not how his people got to know him.

The biblical approach is much better, not only because it is God's own revelation but because it presents us with God as a *person* from the very beginning. And getting to know a person is much more appealing and vital than philosophizing about a First Cause (who ultimately turns out to be a person, for reason can finally lead us to this conclusion).

When God entered into his special relationship with the Hebrews, he began to reveal many things about himself, both by word and action. There was a progression both in the revelation and in the understanding of its meaning. Man's essential knowledge of the one God was fairly complete by the end of the Old Testament. The New Testament chiefly confirms—adds interesting new harmonics or overtones. In the following pages we shall not trace every possible attribute through all of revelation, but we shall sketch the broad outlines of what God meant to the men of the Bible. Once we have this picture clearly in mind, we can move on to how the Church has confirmed it and how reason under the light of faith has tried to come to a more precise philosophical formulation of his nature and attributes. Finally, something will be said about the limitations of man's knowledge of what God is.

THE SCRIPTURAL PICTURE OF GOD

God Is a Living Person

The beauty of the scriptural presentation of God is that he appears from the very beginning as a living person. It will later become the language of Christian theology to speak of three distinct persons in the divine essence, but for the moment the stress is on his personal nature. To Israel, Yahweh seemed "a person." To call him "living" is basic to the Hebrew concept of God: it is an immediate reaction in the face of all he did for them and to them. They are convinced of his life through the power he exercises so strikingly in their behalf. In fact when Yahweh (the personal name he revealed to Moses, Ex 3,14) wishes to confirm threats or promises, he starts by first affirming that he is indeed alive; for example, *"As I live,* I will visit upon his head the oath he has despised and the agreement he has broken" (Ez 17,19).

60   Even before monotheism is firmly established, life is what distinguishes Yahweh from other gods. Israel is sure of the feebleness of

foreign gods in contrast to their living God. (Jer 10, 9f) Some scholars think the title one devised against the nature gods of the gentiles who die and rise with the seasons, whereas Yahweh simply *lives*. The conviction that he is alive rests essentially on the fact that God is not a thing, a force, a power, but a *personal being*. (1 Sm 17,26.36) He is alive because of all the things he does for them, even to being the giver of life itself. (Jer 38,16) Their fondest hope is to be able to approach this living God. (Ps 41[42], 3; 83[84],3) It is their belief in this living God that leads them ultimately to affirm victory over death.

Their realization of God as a living person, acting powerfully in their lives, gives rise to anthropomorphic language. Even the highly spiritual theology of Second Isaia and the New Testament often speaks of him as it would of a living human being. God speaks (Gn 1,3), hears (Ex 16,12), laughs (Ps 2,4; 58[59],9); uses organs suited to these acts: eyes (Am 9,4), hands (Ps 138[139],5), arms (Is 51,9; Jer 27,5), ears (Is 22,14), feet (Na 1,3; Is 63,3) which he places on a footstool. (Is 66,1) Again, God's life is seen in his actions of coming down from heaven (Gn 11,7), shutting the door of the ark (Gn 7,16), and so on. He is shown as having all the human emotions: e.g., disgust (Lv 20,23), regret (Gn 6,6), jealousy. (Ex 20,5; Dt 5,9)

Similar evidence is found in the New Testament, but here Christ deepens the notion of God as a living person by his emphasis on God as a *Father,* not only of Christ himself but of all men (Mt 6,1–32; 7,11; etc.); he is a Father who is concerned about what we eat and wear (Mt 6,25–32), who loves us enough to send his only Son (Jn 3,16) to save us from our sins (Rom 5,8), who wants to make us his own adopted sons (Gal 4,5). He is, moreover, the God who lives and reigns forever. (1 Tim 1,17) He is the life and light of men (Jn 1,4), very light and life itself. (1 Jn 1,5; 5,20)

As the men of the New Testament come to realize that Christ is not just the messenger of God but God himself, they have the final and definitive evidence of God as a living person. Thus the theology of Paul, John, and the primitive Christian Church all proclaim the living God in Christ; the primitive Christian faith encounters in Christ the living God.

God Is All-Powerful

Power impresses. Israel's realization of God's personality, uniqueness, and greatness comes in large measure through the overwhelming
experience of his power. By his power the Hebrews come to know him
first as vastly superior to any other god, then as the only possible God.
True, he tells Abraham even from the start "I am the almighty God"
(Gn 17,1), but it is actions more than words that convinces his people.
The theme of power is therefore a constant one running through all the
other ideas of God.

God picks out a weak nation with little to recommend it, yet with
his help it is able to do the impossible. He frees them from the bondage
of powerful Egypt, establishes them in the Promised Land, and repeatedly helps them overcome their enemies. At first his people seem
to think of him as supreme within Israel itself; but slowly there dawns
the realization that his power extends to the ends of the earth.

At least in the latter part of the Old Testament God is clearly
seen as Creator and absolute Lord of the whole universe. With a sign
he calls into being the heavens, earth, and seas; he cares for all things,
and unless he sustains them they fall back into nothingness. (Wis 11,26)
He holds in his hands the destiny of all mankind. He has power over
all nations (Nm 21,3; 1 Sm 14,12ff), he can drive the king of Assyria
to chastise his people, then halt him, powerless, before the walls of
Jerusalem. (4 Kgs 19,35) That God permits his people to be led into
exile is recognized as punishment for infidelity; it is not due to any lack
of power.

The New Testament simply takes for granted God's almighty
power; nothing is impossible to him. (Mt 19,26; Lk 1,37)

God Is One

Abraham's ancestors were pagans and polytheists. So, even after
God revealed himself to him (Gn 17), it probably took Abraham and
his descendants a long time to understand just how unique this God was.

62   The first clear affirmation of God's oneness is made through Moses:
"I, the Lord, am your God . . . you shall not have other gods besides

me." (Ex 20,2f) Yet even after this there is some evidence that the Hebrews have not understood completely. They know that this is an absolute prohibition against worshipping any other gods, but belief in the existence of other gods for other nations lingered on. (1 Sm 26,19; 4 Kgs 3,27) Even in David's time it was presumed that Yahweh's power ended at the frontiers of Israel. (1 Sm 26,19; Mi 4,5) For Israel in her earliest period, however, two things are already clear: Yahweh is *the* God of Israel, and he is the *supreme* god.

Little by little it becomes evident to the people through Yahweh's manifestation of power that he is not only superior to any other god, but totally unique. Moses confounds the gods of Egypt; foreign gods are seen as powerless to help their nations (e.g., 4 Kgs 18,33ff).

It is thanks to the work of the prophets, particularly, that the Hebrews outgrow any tendency to think of Yahweh as God of Israel only. They preach the Lord as creator of all, God of the whole world and of all history, as well as of the chosen people. Thus Deuteronomy has the classic formula, "Yahweh is God and there is no other God but him." (4,35; 6,4; 32,39)[1] Jeremia speaks of foreign gods as gods "who are not gods at all!" (2,11; 5,7) And Second Isaia puts the final touches on the notion of monotheism. In proclaiming the almighty power of Yahweh (41,1–4) he asserts that other gods not only have no power but are really nonexistent; he calls them "nonentities," empty breath, human creations which have no reality other than the material of which their idols are fashioned. (43,10ff; 44,6ff; 45,20ff)

Although the New Testament was to reveal the trinity of persons in God, Christ wishes to build upon the solid foundation of faith in the one God. When asked about the first of the commandments, he repeats the ancient formula "Hear, O Israel! Yahweh is our God, Yahweh alone," (Mk 12,29) or "The Lord our God is one God," as the post-Christian rabbis came to translate this phrase of Dt 6,4, making it a more explicitly monotheistic formula. St. Paul, in explaining the unity of the Church says there is but "one Lord, one faith, one baptism, one God." (Eph 4,5f) And St. John reports our Lord's words, that everlasting life consists in knowing "the only true God. . . ." (Jn 17,3) The very

---

[1] Deuteronomy in its final form (not its sources) dates from after the exile, fifth century b.c., hence the clarity.

reason, it seems, why Christ revealed the mystery of his own divine status and that of the Paraclete so slowly was in order not to undermine the deep and abiding faith of Israel in the one true God.

God Is Eternal

Whereas other religions always presented a theogony (genealogy of the gods) as a first step in the organization of chaos, there is no trace of speculation among the Hebrews about the origin of God. Yahweh has no history, no consort (there is no Hebrew word for "goddess"), no family; he is just there from the start. His preexistence and endless continuance are taken for granted. The world has a beginning, God has none. "Before the mountains were brought forth and the earth and the world were born, from eternity to eternity, thou art, O God! for a thousand years in your sight are as yesterday which has passed, as a watch in the night." (Ps 89[90],2) Creative power is seen to imply eternal (or better, everlasting) existence. (Jb 38,4ff; Prv 8,22ff) God's everlasting life continues to be expressed more and more emphatically. (Jer 10,10; Is 43,13; Dn 12,7)

The Hebrews, of course, were not thinking philosophically about this term; Yahweh's eternity meant that his end and beginning were forever clouded by the unknown. The mysterious name "Yahweh" (related to "I am": "He who is," or "He who causes to be"), implied life in unending actuality. The Hebrews do not have to be philosophers to grasp the significance of "He who is" as compared with the ephemeral nature of the seasons and years, the grass of the desert which withers so fast, the flocks which are born and die, and men whose bodies soon return to dust.

In the New Testament our Lord insinuates his divinity by appealing to his eternity. (Jn 8,58) St. Paul speaks of God as "King of ages, God immortal." (1 Tim 1,17) St. John gives us the expression reminiscent of Second Isaia: "I am the Alpha and the Omega, the beginning and the end, who is, who was and who is coming." (Ap 1,8; cf. Is 41,4; 48,12)

God Is Everywhere Present and Near

Once God entered into the dialogue of familiarity with his people, Israel's desire was to come to know this personal God as closely as possible; and knowledge in its deepest sense meant proximity, love, and communion. The sacred authors and prophets continually impress upon the people that God is not far off and remote—as they thought when building the golden calf (Ex 32ff)—but a God who is ever near. "What great nation is there that has gods so close to it as the Lord, our God, is to us whenever we call upon him?" (Dt 4,7)

Even in the earliest books, God is seen as truly with his people, mingling in their lives, speaking to them, visiting Abraham. Israel is even seen as his "son," his "first-born." (Ex 4,22) Osea portrays God as a tender father. (11,1ff) In the later writings of the Old Testament the personal closeness with God is depicted by individual conversations with him. (Ps 35[36],8ff; 41[42],2; 71[72],1ff) One theory would even translate "Yahweh" precisely as "He who is present" to his people.

Once the notion of God as creator became clear, the Israelites began to realize that God is not only present to them, but present everywhere. Solomon acknowledges that if the heavens cannot contain God, how much less the temple he has built. (3 Kgs 8,27) God's omnipresence is beautifully expressed in Ps 138[139],8ff: "Where can I go from your spirit? from your presence where can I flee? If I go up to the heavens, you are there; if I sink down to the nether world, you are present there. If I take the wings of the dawn, if I settle at the farthest limits of the sea, even there your hand shall guide me, and your right hand hold me fast."

It was for the New Testament to complete this notion of God's omnipresence with that of his immanence; that is, that God is not only present *to* all things, but present *in* all things. Thus his true omnipresence means more than a vague overshadowing of the whole world. St. Paul is particularly clear about the "one God and Father of us all, who is above all, and throughout all and in us all." (Eph 4,6) God is so present to us that "in him we live and move and have our being." (Ac 17,28)

God Is "Completely Other," Unchangeable, a Spirit

One-sided insistence upon God's immanence can lead to pantheism, the view that God is not personally distinct from man and the world. But if the men of the Bible are aware of God's presence, they are even more conscious of the fundamental distinction between God and man: that the distance is in fact infinite. God is, then, "completely other," or transcendent.

Though many anthropomorphic expressions are used to show God's closeness, and especially that he is a living person inviting us to personal relationship, nonetheless he remains wholly other. He is not a man but God. (Os 11,9) This "otherness" of God is recognized in his *unchangeableness*. "I am the Lord and I change not." (Mal 3,6) Everything else is fickle and changing, but not God. (Nm 23,19; Ps 101[102],27f)

So aware are the men of the Old Testament that human expressions simply cannot capture the divine personality that they forbid any visual representations of Yahweh. To make an image of God to them meant to want to imprison him within certain limits—something that their awareness of God's transcendence clearly forbids. In fact the sense of divine "otherness" grows steadily deeper in Israel's religion, till it comes to eliminate the very name "Yahweh," the proper, sacred, and dread name of their God, the name revealed to Moses. According to the Semitic mind, the name is part of the mystery of the being who is named. In the third century B.C. "Adonai" (my Lord) began to be substituted in public readings.

The real basis for this "otherness" and unchangeableness of God, this big difference between God and men, is given us by Isaia: namely, the one is Spirit, the other flesh. (31,3) But the ancient religions have always had trouble with the notion of pure spirituality; the gods of all religions appeared to be corporeal in some way, with bodies and actions often resembling man's. It is debatable whether the men of the Bible escape this conception entirely. Even the Book of Isaia (40,13 and 31,3) is affirming more the power and immortality of God than what we would call his spiritual nature.

66   The New Testament increases the understanding of spirituality. Jesus tells the Samaritan woman, for example, that no material building

is needed to worship God, since "God is spirit, and those who worship him should worship him in spirit and truth." (Jn 4,24) Christ is not here talking about God's being devoid of body and matter; rather he states that while God is spirit (deity, we would say) there is also, at the highest level of man's being, a "spirit" of man, and that on this high level (whatever it is) man best communes with God. It was to be the work of theology to pinpoint exactly this notion of the spirituality of God.

God Is Holy

The transcendence or "complete otherness" of God is most clearly expressed in the Bible by the notion of holiness. God is holy. He is "the holy one." (Is 5,24) This is the most characteristic note of God for the men of the Bible. Holiness in God does not imply, however, effort or struggle against evil. It is more than a moral perfection: it signifies a mystery of absolute perfection and inaccessibility.

Certainly, God is pure, sacred, and untouchable, completely exempt from all faults, sins, or vices. From this results God's hatred of sin, and his punishment of evil. (Is 42,25; Ez 28,22) But the holiness of God is primarily a positive thing, absolute perfection. So much does it separate him from all creatures that even the seraphim must cover their faces as they sing "Holy, holy, holy." (Is 6,3) He is "other" to the point of unapproachableness.

Thus, no matter how closely men are in touch with God, they are aware that the secret of God's own being can never be encroached upon. From this there flows the natural attitude of "fear of the Lord" so often seen in the Old Testament. Indeed this awe which is reverent fear, not craven fear, is the "beginning of the knowledge of God." (Ps 110[111],10; Prv 1,7; Jb 28,28)

The positive side of holiness is expressed by majesty and glory. Glory is the radiant power of his being, a sort of external manifestation of his mysterious holiness; this glory radiates over all heaven and earth. (Is 6,3) The New Testament account of the transfiguration of Christ is a striking example of this radiance of God's holiness. The Apostles fall to the ground overwhelmed by the evidence of his holiness and glory. (Mt 17,1ff)

Transcendence, glory, majesty, unapproachableness serve to underline the uniqueness of God. This explains the *jealous* God sometimes mentioned (Ex 20,5; Ez 39,25), who cannot share his glory with anyone else. (Is 42,8; 43,11) This jealousy can take the form of wrath, both against the pagans (Jer 25,15ff) and against the people of Israel. (Is 5,25; 9,7ff; Jer 15,14; Nm 25,11)

The New Testament relieves some of the unapproachableness of God by the emphasis on God as a loving and tender father, because the men of the New Testament came to know God in Christ. They are nonetheless as aware of the absolute holiness of God as their fathers had been. (Jn 17,11; I Jn 2,20; Ap 4,8)

THEOLOGICAL CLARIFICATIONS
ON THE NATURE OF GOD

The Teaching of the Church

Belief in the one God who is infinite and perfect has been so firmly held by Christianity that there is little need to trace the repeated expressions of this faith in the Fathers of the Church and Councils. The biggest opposition has been in the form of pantheism, the doctrine which draws creatures and God so closely together that it ends by identifying them. The scientific pantheism of Spinoza, for example, is a type of monism that reduces all reality to spirit and its activity; reality is one substance manifesting itself in two manners: extension and thought; or as matter (the world) and spirit (God). Another variation is the idealistic pantheism of Hegel which teaches that God is within the material world itself, the vital force urging it on to ever more perfect realization. For Hegel, this absolute is envisaged as Future Humanity; it is not yet a reality, but a perennial becoming. The error of the pantheists is in not seeing God as completely distinct from the world (a distinction guaranteed by the Christian notion of creation), and as eternally perfect and unchangeable.

It is with this in mind that the I Vatican Council sums up the traditional teaching on the nature of God. "The Church . . . believes and professes that there is one true and living God, the creator and lord of heaven and earth. He is all-powerful, eternal, unmeasurable, incomprehensible, and infinite in intellect and will and in every perfection. Since he is one unique spiritual substance, entirely simple and unchangeable, he must be really and essentially distinct from the world, perfectly happy both in himself and by his very nature, inexpressibly exalted over all things that exist or can be conceived other than himself." (D1782)

Dealing with specific pantheistic doctrines, the Council added condemnations against those who say,

(a) that finite things, both corporal and spiritual, or at least spiritual, emanate from the divine substance;

(b) that the divine essence becomes all things by a manifestation or evolution of itself;

(c) finally, that God is universal or indefinite being, which by determining itself makes up a universe diversified into genera, species, and individuals. (D1804)

In the defined teaching of the Church summed up at the I Vatican Council, the attributes of God are presented in biblical terms and are to be understood according to the language of Scripture from which they are borrowed. God is *one,* as opposed to multiple (polytheism); God is *true,* as opposed to nonexistent, illusory, or unfaithful to his word; God is *living,* as opposed to inert. This is a God, then, who possesses an intimate life and who acts, one with whom one can enter into true relations.

The Council then enumerates four perfections which theologians consider to be intimately bound up with the essence of God: eternity, immensity, incomprehensibility, and infinity. The theological understanding of these will be treated presently.

In the last section of the chapter (D1782 above), the Council is opposing pantheism by pointing out the "otherness" of God. The distinction between him and the world is called *real* (that is, not just a mental distinction, as between man and rational animal, nor a virtual one, as between the mercy and justice of God), and *essential* (that is, resulting from the very nature of God, who is not merely distinct from the world as one individual thing is distinct from another of the same species, but as one being is distinct from another whose nature is absolutely different from its own).

Finally, to say that the divine substance is *unique* signifies that God and the world do not form a kind of composite; in other words, God cannot be conceived as the soul of the world. It also means that the divine substance is not the same as that of the world, as if the world itself were divine and all things in it simply emanations from the one divine substance. In this way the Council rejects all forms of pantheism. Insistence upon the *simplicity* and *unchangeableness* of God further show the impossibility of pantheism being true.

The Nature or Essence of God

The basic facts about God's nature and attributes are not mysteries. Human reason can arrive at them if it is rightly used. With regard to the one God reason can demonstrate, as well as throw a certain light upon, the facts we have received from Scripture and the Church. However, the process of philosophical demonstration is quite different from that of receiving a revelation. Some would say (Karl Barth, for example) that the two are absolutely incompatible as ways of knowing God, the former leading only to the answer to a philosophical problem, the latter to the living God; but the Church holds in honor a true "theology of God," namely a metaphysical inquiry into the biblical data.

The men of the Bible are not interested in philosophical reasoning about God; they know him first as a person and gradually come to a full knowledge of all his attributes. (For them, however, the latter are more the "attitudes" of God in his dealings with them.) They have little concern with finding out just what is the "essence" of this divine person.

Reason leads to the discovery of the same God; but the philosopher discovers—not without much difficulty—the same facts that faith teaches about God's nature and attributes. Starting with the data of the classic arguments for the existence of God, he first discovers the *nature* of God, or that notion from which all else must necessarily flow. The individual attributes then follow upon this logically, such as simplicity, perfection, and so on. Only toward the end of the process can the philosopher come to the notion of the *personal* God.[2]

---

[2] For this reason we have deliberately left the philosophical treatment to the end; for to know God as soon as possible as *personal* is essential if our relationship with God is to be seen as personal encounter.

What then is the basic notion of God from which all else flows? Gabriel Marcel would define God as the "Absolute Thou," because he is the person to whom one commits oneself entirely. Still, for the philosopher this is not evident at the outset. Kant sees God as primarily the Just Judge demanded by our appetite for justice. But again this is putting things in reverse. Plato's God is the Good, essentially; Anselm's and Descartes' the Perfect Being than whom no greater can be conceived. But for the majority of Catholic theologians God is best defined as *self-subsisting being* (*ipsum esse subsistens*), since his "whatness" is identified with his very being or existence (*esse*). (*S. Th.*, 1ª,3,4; *S.C.G.*, 1, 21–22) St. Thomas sees this as the culmination point of the five ways. The reasoning is as follows.

The *prime mover* can explain its own activity only by being *pure act* in the order of operation. It must then be the same in the order of being itself (entitative order); for how one acts follows from what one is. God's essence, then, is not only capable of existing (as with us), but must be its own act of existence, or *self-subsisting being*. In other words, since in God there is no potentiality, it follows that in him essence does not differ from existence. His essence must necessarily and of itself exist.

Second, the *first cause* must find within itself the reason for its own existence. It cannot cause itself, for to do so it would have to be in existence already. Thus it does not receive existence, but *is* this very existence.

Third, the very notion of *necessary being* implies existence as essential to it; this means that it must not only have existence but that it must be its very existence. Fourth, the *perfect being* cannot merely participate in existence or being, any more than it can merely participate in goodness or truth. It must *be* them. Thus there is no distinction between its essence as a limiting principle and its existence as limited, or of essence capable of existence and an existence actualizing or determining this essence. Last, the *first intelligence* (i.e., orderer of all things) which directs all things to their goals cannot itself be directed to perfection or being as to an object distinct from itself. It must be being itself, always known to itself. (See R. Garrigou-Lagrange, *God, His Existence and Nature,* tr. Bede Rose, O.S.B. [St. Louis: B. Herder, 1934], II, 19ff.)

The most basic thing that can be said about God, therefore, is that he is self-subsisting being. This may be called his essence. Not only is this notion the culminating point in the ascending order of reasoning from the five ways, but it is also the starting point or principle in the descending order, from which all the necessary attributes of God can be deduced.

Many writers describe God's essence simply as *aseity,* or *absolute self-sufficiency* (aseity: the property of that which exists of itself and in virtue of itself; that is, God being *"a se"* signifies that he is completely sufficient to himself, that he needs nothing outside himself to explain his own actuality). There is little to choose between these two definitions of God's essence. Certainly the latter is demanded by the former: self-sufficiency by self-subsisting being; but self-subsisting being is preferable, since it is a more positive notion, and does not imply in any way that God causes himself (something that might seem implied in aseity).

The Attributes of God

A divine attribute is defined as an absolutely simple perfection which exists in God necessarily according to its proper form and which, according to our imperfect way of knowing it, is deduced from what we know as the divine essence. Goodness, truth, and simplicity are examples of absolutely simple perfections; they imply no admixture of imperfection.

On the other hand, rationality and health are perfections that are not simple, since the former implies laborious mental processes rather than immediate vision of things, and the latter implies a material being subject to sickness and decomposition. Such relative perfections are said to exist in God only virtually (that is, insofar as he has the power, *virtus,* to make them exist in us). Furthermore, things like creation and providence are not considered divine attributes, since they result from a *free* act of God and are not irrevocably bound up with his essence.

The human mind divides these attributes into those which relate to the *being* of God and those which relate to the *divine operations.* With a beautiful display of logical deduction, St. Thomas (and others before and after) shows how each of these many attributes flows from 72 the essence of God. (*S. Th.,* 1ª, qq. 3–25; and especially *S.C.G.,* 1,15– 102) Under the attributes related to the being of God, we shall treat briefly God's unity, simplicity, infinite perfection, omnipresence, unchangeableness, and eternity. A separate chapter will be necessary to treat the attributes related to the divine operations: God's intelligence, will, and (granted his free decision to create) providence and the act of creation.

Individual Attributes Related to God's Being

UNITY   This, like all the others, is a necessary conclusion from self-subsisting being. The act of being, considered in its absolute purity, simply cannot admit of multiplicity. There cannot be two acts of pure being; for the only thing that could distinguish the second from the first would be some perfection not possessed by the first one—which is impossible. The classic proofs for God's existence, then, lead us at once to the philosophical verification of the monotheism already so clear in Scripture and defined by the Church.

SIMPLICITY   Granted that God is one, is there any composition in him? Everything else we know is composed of parts: man, trees, tiny cells, even the atom. Complexity is not a virtue in philosophy, which dearly loves to reduce all things to unity. It attains its desire for ultimate unity in the notion of God.

The men of the Bible knew that God was totally "other" than creatures and even came to the knowledge that "God is spirit." (Jn 4,24) But they probably never saw the ultimate ramifications of simplicity. The Fathers of the Church, however, arrive at the concept of absolute incorporeality and deny all composition. They declare, for example, that God is the most incorporeal being, the most purely immaterial and the simplest that exists. Even faced with the difficulties raised by the doctrine of the Trinity, they had no hesitation in maintaining the unity and simplicity of God.

To explain further the simplicity of God we must take things we know and show that all the various kinds of composition we find in created things must be denied of God: composition of matter and form, such as our bodies and souls; composition of substance and accidents, such as a tree with its characteristics of size, shape, color; and finally even composition of essence and existence, for example, composition of   73 what makes John a man rather than a tree or stone (essence), and what makes him exist (existence).

Even angels, though incorporeal, are composites of substance and accidents (intellect and will are accidental to them), and of essence and existence. Ultimately no created thing *has* to exist; that is, its "whatness" is not necessarily connected with its "to be" or existence. When it comes into being there is immediately the basic composition of essence and existence.

All composition is reducible to potency and act; but in God there is no way in which he can be perfected. He *has* nothing, *acquires* nothing, because he *is* infinite being. Putting it philosophically, God is entirely simple because he is pure act.

In attempting to find ultimate unity, some thinkers have fallen into pantheism which recognizes the divine in all things, saying that somehow God is identified with the totality of the world—as its "soul" perhaps, or as the one substance from which all other things emanate. But this would destroy the simplicity of God since it would mean some kind of composition; it would also militate against the unchangeableness of God. These reasons, as well as the doctrine of creation, lie behind the strong words of the I Vatican Council condemning pantheism. (D1804)

God transcends the universe; he is completely above it. This notion has nothing to do with space or distance. It relates to the absolute independence, the total self-sufficiency, and the perfect aseity of God.

INFINITE PERFECTION   Scripture has shown us God as the summit of all good things; whether in regard to power or truth or holiness he is the ultimate. He is, in brief, perfect. (Mt 5,48) The Church says simply, he is "infinite in every perfection." (D1782)

A thing is still imperfect if it has not yet reached the highest possible degree of attainment, if there is still present some unactualized potential. A "perfect stone" has far less perfection than "a perfect man," however, because it had far less potential to start with. God would be imperfect if he could still become something he is not, or possess something he does not yet have; but once we realize that he is subsisting being itself, pure actuality, we begin to see how he is complete to the point of infinity. There is no limitation whatsoever in his essence. It does not ever lack existence. It necessarily *is*.

74

Again we can understand something of the infinity of God's perfection by taking all the possible perfections of this world such as mercy, love, justice, goodness—and attributing them to God infinitely, without limitation.

OMNIPRESENCE   The simplicity and spirituality of God help us to understand omnipresence. In fact, for the author of Wisdom, it is this very simplicity of God which enables him to be everywhere present. (Wis 1,7) Being simple, he is unextended in any material way and not subject to any measurement.

Omnipresence gives us the notion of what is unmeasurable, infinite as regards space. Abstracting from all creation, this is the attribute of *immensity* defined by the Church (D1782); but in terms of creation, place, and space, we say God is omnipresent.

This attribute can most easily be grasped in reference to causality. God is necessarily the first cause of all that exists. Things only come into existence and retain existence by a continual influx of creative power. God is present through his very essence as well as his power, for all is one in God. This presence not only *to* all things, but *in* all things (Ac 17,28; Eph 4,6) is called *immanence*. It is not a vague mingling of the divine being with created things, but rather a mode of spiritual presence not reducible to any kind of bodily presence, thus something infinitely more intimate, penetrating, and close.[3]

A correct notion of God's immanence points up the fallacy of deism, the error which holds that once God creates the world he is no longer concerned with it, leaving it to run its inevitable course. The deists are wrong on a number of counts. They know neither the living personal God of revelation nor the same immanent God of true philosophy.

UNCHANGEABLENESS   Best expressed by the words "no change or shadow of alteration" in James 1,17, and the "immutable" of the I Vatican Council (D1782), this concept remains very difficult to grasp.

---

[3] Onesided insistence on immanence leads to the pantheism discussed previously; for pantheism is based on the deep awareness of God *within* creation. All the ancient mythologies and pagan metaphysics rest upon a confusion between the order of the created and the uncreated, the confusion between the world and the Absolute. (C. Tresmontant, "Biblical Metaphysics," *Cross Currents,* 10 [Summer, 1960], 234)

God is a *living* person, yet change is part of every life as we know it.

In created things change (at its best) is a ceaseless effort toward perfection. Living things are able to change for the better precisely because they are not yet all they could be. If we could conceive of a living thing attaining its state of perfect existence, its life would not cease (for life itself is a perfection), but would be ceaseless life on that perfect, unchanging level.

So with God. His is not the unchangeableness of a rock, but the unchangeableness of perfect life. He is everything which can be, to the point of being identified with existence and life itself. His actuality consists in being, totally and absolutely. Because of his absolute, unlosable perfection, he is unchangeable and immobile. He is above change rather than beneath it, not deprived of change, but above change. (See A. M. Henry, ed., *God and His Creation*, pp. 70-73.)

ETERNITY   The eternal existence of God is clearly affirmed in Scripture. But the Hebrew word as used, for example, in Psalm 89[90], 2-4, does not contain all the nuances that later theology will see in the term. Its original meaning designated something hidden, a secret duration, whose beginning and end are forever clouded by the unknown. As defined by the Church in its various creeds, it certainly means *without* beginning or end.

However, theologians go somewhat farther than the defined doctrine, in accepting the definition of Boethius. The sixth century philosopher (d. 524) explains that not only has eternity no beginning or end, but it implies no succession of time or events. "Eternity is the total, simultaneous, and perfect possession of life without end." (*On the Consolation of Philosophy*, 5,6)

Created things are subject to change and movement; one event succeeds another. Time is the measure of this succession or motion, in terms of a before and after. We are perfectly aware of it when we speak of doing one thing after we finish another. But God's eternity implies none of this. Just as his omnipresence gives him infinitude with regard to space, so eternity gives him infinitude with regard to time. There is not even any succession of thoughts in God (as there is in the case of us and the angels). All in God is one eternal act of knowledge and love.

76

Why? Because he has complete simplicity, even his intelligence and will and their acts are identical with his being.

Conclusion

The picture of what God is is still not complete. The next chapter will treat of the activity of God, or his active attributes of intellect and will. Only then can natural theology say that God is alive, active, a *personal* God. Only then does the rational picture of God rejoin the revealed picture which starts out with God as a person.

Even if human reason did not know of divine personality from revelation, she could still arrive at it by her own resources. Philosophy can demonstrate that the divine essence subsists in itself as infinite personality. It can prove that God is not just a thing, but an "I." God is a person, a living, knowing, willing, and loving *ego* whom one cannot, except unjustly, treat as a thing. If the Church has not defined the personality of the one God, it is only because of the danger of confusion; for as the volume on the Trinity will explain, God is not just one person but three.[4]

CLARIFICATIONS
REGARDING OUR KNOWLEDGE OF GOD

Distinction of Attributes Is Due to Human Weakness

How is it possible to assert that God is completely simple, that there is no composition whatever in him, and yet discuss each attribute in turn as if it were distinct and different? Is theology being inconsistent? No. We must hold that there is no *real* distinction of parts or attributes in God. In us many things that are always found together are nonetheless not the same: soul is not body, eyes are not ears, our nature or "whatness" is not our existence or "to be." This is not the case with God.

If *real* distinction were the only possible kind, we would end up in near-agnosticism. We would be able to say nothing about God. But fortunately we can also make valid distinctions *of reason.* One kind is

[4] A good treatment of how reason can prove the personality of God is found in J. Daniélou, *God and the Ways of Knowing,* pp. 69-80.

purely logical, a pure construction of reason; for example, that which we make between man and rational animal. Here the concept remains the same, only the name changes. But the other kind of distinction of reason is more useful, and is used in talking about God: namely, one which has a foundation in reality as we know it. For example, according to our way of seeing things, mercy is different from justice, knowing from loving, and so on. Since the concepts are different, we come to some real and worthwhile knowledge in applying them to God. Nor do we apply them to him arbitrarily, for he himself has justified such usage: Scripture is filled with God's revelation of himself in our terms. Nowhere is language more concrete and adapted to the weakness of man's way of knowing than in the inspired writings. The distinctions we make in God are known as *virtual* distinctions.

We are able to think about infinite being only by a multiplicity of concepts; to approach it at all we are obliged to fragmentize or refract, so to speak, the infinite richness. The human mind cannot reflect upon the idea of God except piecemeal, cannot use it in its oneness and entirety. The divine attributes, then, express the aspects under which God can be conceived by the human intelligence. All is one in God. All the separate things and dogmas we can define about him actually have their meeting point in the one undivided godhead. Each attribute implies all the others. Only if we fully understood one of them would we be able to comprehend at the same time all the others—and in fact God himself. It is for this reason—though without understanding it—that it is more correct to say that God *is* subsisting goodness, love, intelligence, than to say he *has* goodness, love, intelligence. For ultimately they are not parts or facets of God but are identified with the divine substance.

God Is Incomprehensible

Man never will or can comprehend God. In fact, even to speak of him is to attempt the impossible: the finite trying to understand the infinite. Scripture cautions, "Mortal man cannot see me and live to tell of it" (Ex 33,20); and St. Paul cries out, "How deep is the mine of God's wisdom and of his knowledge; how inscrutable are his judgments, and how unsearchable his ways! Who has ever understood the Lord's thought or been his counsellor?" (Rom 11,33)

78

St. Augustine realized the difficulty of attempting to say things positively about God; but if we cannot understand what he is, at least we can conceive of what he is not. He is not body, earth, heaven, sun, not any bodily thing. And so we rise to the notion of God as pure spirit. (*On John,* Homily 23,9) With all his marvellous writing, St. Thomas says we know God as one unknown. We know he exists, but not really what he is; we know better what he is not. (*Concerning Boethius on the Trinity,* 1,2,2)

Even in heaven, with the help of the light of glory, we shall not fully comprehend God. Never will the infinite be encompassed by the finite. The Vatican Council sums up the traditional teaching of the Church in defining God as incomprehensible. (D1782)

Man's Knowledge of God Is Analogous, Thus True but Imperfect

All knowledge of God in this life is by analogy; that is, by the use of notions or concepts—such as personality, beauty, goodness—applied to God in a way that is partially the same as, and partially different from, the way they are applied to finite things. *Causality, negation,* and *eminence* are the three ways to this analogous knowledge. A short application of these to the notion of personality in God may prove helpful.

Having demonstrated that God is the first cause of all things, one may ask "Well, is he a person, or just a thing?" We know what personality is in man: that which allows one to be an independent, thinking, rational substance. It is man's highest gift, and we are persons somehow because we are spiritual beings. Now from this, the *way of causation* leads us to say that personality must exist in God. For if this perfection —and it is that—is found in the creature, it is only possible if the Creator had it before him.[5]

Still, there are some things about human persons which we cannot attribute to God's personality: need of a body, individualistic traits, likes and dislikes, imperfections, and so on. But it seems possible to eliminate

---

[5] God is not, by the same token, however, a tree or animal, since they imply deficiencies: lack of sensation, lack of true intellective power. But excellent qualities which imply no lack, which look as though they could be multiplied indefinitely, are those which belong to God, e.g., truth, mercy.

these without disturbing the basic notion of "I"-ness in God. All the imperfections with which created things are mixed must be strained out. This is the *way of negation*.

God is a person, then, but not a person in the finite, creaturely sense. We must complete this by using one more step: the *way of eminence*. By this is not meant simply a higher grade of goodness, mercy, and so on, in God, and thus a more perfect personality. To say that someone is eminently suited to lead the Democratic Party means he is much better suited than others. But here the word "eminent" has lost much of its depth by being overworked (as have also the words infinite, divine, and the like). When we say that personality is to be eminently attributed to God, we mean in a quite different sense from the way we see it in creatures, a difference not just of degree, but of kind. It means that God has personality in a way that is utterly unimaginable to us.

The same process of analogy holds true in saying that God is beautiful. We are saying three things: he is beautiful, or he could not have created a world of beauty; he is not beautiful in the way in which we conceive of it—in terms of lines, form, colors, harmony; he is infinitely or eminently beautiful in a way simply unimaginable to us—to the point of beauty being identical with his very substance. (See R. Knox, *The Hidden Stream* [London: Burns Oates, 1952], p. 29-38.) This is knowledge by analogy, a process which gives us true but imperfect knowledge of God. It is a process first used by God in revealing himself to us in the Scriptures.

CREATION

"In the beginning God created the heavens and the earth. . . . God made the two great lights, the greater light to rule the day, and the small one to rule the night, and he made the stars." (Gn 1,1.16)

CHAPTER THREE

GOD'S ACTIVITY

God has revealed himself as living, active, personal. But what does God do? Obviously he does not grow, reproduce, or carry on any of the activities which require a body or matter. God's activity is that of a completely spiritual being, namely, intellection and volition: the only operations not intrinsically bound to matter. Thus all activity in God is reducible to acts involving the intellect, the will, or both. We shall treat successively the divine knowledge, the divine will, divine providence and predestination, and finally the act of creation.

DIVINE KNOWLEDGE

Scripture

Almost every page of the Bible teaches that God knows. He knows the goodness of his creative activity; he knows the sin of Adam and Eve as soon as it is committed; he knows that Sara laughed to herself on hearing she was to bear a child in her old age (Gn 18,12f); he unveils the future to Joseph. (Gn 40–41) The Psalms are filled with the idea that God knows all things: "O Lord, you have probed me and you know me; you know when I sit and when I stand; you understand my thoughts from afar. . . . Even before a word is on my tongue, behold, O Lord, you know the whole of it." (Ps 138[139],1–4) God knows all things because he is their creator (Ps 32[33],13f), and surely he who creates eyes to see is able himself to see all. (Ps 93[94],9ff)

The New Testament confirms the fact that God's knowledge extends to the most secret and smallest things. He sees in secret (Mt 6,18) and he knows our prayer even before it is uttered. (Mt 6,8) From the most trivial things—the number of hairs of our head (Mt 10,30)—to the most important—the date of the end of the world (Mt 24,36)— nothing escapes his omniscience.[1] When Christ begins to reveal the Trinity, he tells us that what God knows most of all is himself: "No one knows the Son except the Father; nor does anyone know the Father except the Son, and him to whom the Son chooses to reveal him." (Mt 11,27; Lk 10,22) St. Paul explains: "For who among men knows the things of a man save the spirit of the man which is in him? Even so, the things of God no one knows but the Spirit of God." (1 Cor 2,11)

---

[1] Omniscience is indeed a conclusion of theodicy about God. But this is a good example of what Karl Rahner calls God revealing his *attitudes* toward man rather than just attributes. In other words, the biblical account reveals the attributes of God with new harmonics, new overtones, because they are seen in terms of an encounter, a personal contact. Thus, for example, omniscience no longer signifies strictly the infinite consciousness of the world-cause, containing all things in its being and knowledge, but rather the eye of the *personal* God, whose discerning, comprehending, and provident gaze penetrates man's inmost heart and is felt there by him. Mt 6, 4–32; Lk 16,15; I Thes 2,4; 1 Jn 3,20; Heb 4,12f) (See K. Rahner, *art. cit.*, p. 113.)

Theology

The Fathers of the Church had no hesitation about declaring God's infinite wisdom and knowledge, and that even the secrets of the heart are plain to him. When the I Vatican Council defined that God "is perfect in intelligence" (D1782), it was only reiterating a long-standing truth of faith. Reason enlightened by faith now tries to understand this act of divine knowledge, the object of the knowledge, and the special problem of how to reconcile God's knowledge of future free acts with man's freedom.

THE ACT OF DIVINE KNOWLEDGE   The act of knowledge in God is identical with his substance. Why? We must go back a bit to answer this. It can be seen without difficulty that since God is the cause of intelligence in men, he must himself possess intelligence, in a perfect manner and apart from all imperfections of created intellects. Still, if we do not attribute a perfect eye to God, why a perfect intelligence? Because the eye is a material thing and only needed to make up for an imperfection in our way of knowing. Because we do not intuit we must first obtain impressions and images from the outside by means of the five senses. We drink in, possess images of things through the senses: for example, all sorts of impressions about various people. From these data the intellect is able to abstract concepts or ideas, such as the concept of human nature.

To know and to reason and to possess things intellectually is one of man's greatest gifts. The more perfectly one is able to know, the more perfect one is. In a sense, we can possess, make our own, the very things we know: we draw them within us in images and concepts. We even "possess" ourselves by our reflexive thought. However, many imperfections remain. We do all this only in small steps, and laboriously; we possess things very imperfectly, not in themselves but only their images and concepts. But if in God such imperfections and limitations are removed, we can begin to see the possibility of his actually being identified with what he possesses intellectually. This is the idea of infinite being itself. In God the act of knowledge is not a mere adjunct to his person, to his existence, not a potency that is actuated. It is not turned on and off like ours. It is identical with his existence. *83*

Again, all this is demanded by God's simplicity. There are no multiple acts of knowledge in him. Just as we admire the perfection of the intellectual giant who can take so much in in a single glance, think so fast, and compress so much into a single expression, so God in an infinitely more perfect way comprehends all possible knowledge in one single, eternal act of the intellect that is identical with his being. So, it is really more accurate to say that God *is* infinite knowledge than that he has it. He does not produce it in any way; it is not distinct from his essence, not a mere adjunct or accident. God's act of knowledge is substantial, identical with his very being.

OBJECT OF GOD'S KNOWLEDGE   The primary object of God's knowledge is himself. There is no real distinction between his act of knowing and his act of being. By necessarily existing, he also necessarily knows himself perfectly. The secondary object of God's knowledge is all things other than God. He does not have to look at individual things in order to know them; by perfectly understanding himself, infinite being, he sees the limitless possibilities of created and finite participation in being. For this reason theologians more commonly say that God knows all things not in themselves, but in himself.

To look at it another way, *our* knowledge is caused by the things we know, whereas with God the reverse is true: *His* knowledge is the cause of things. Not that every possible participation in the divine essence comes into being, for God must first will their existence. Nonetheless, he knows all that he will ever cause to exist, that is, all the *actuals:* past, present, and future.[2] His knowledge also extends to the *possibles,* namely, all things which could very well exist but never will, simply because God does not wish to create them.

God, then, knows from eternity how we will freely choose to act in the future, when we could as well do the opposite. "All is naked and open to his eyes" (Heb 4,13), "even those things that are going to occur by the free action of creatures." (D1784)

God knows future things and events because he is their cause. But

---

[2] For "Thomists," as the school of D. Bañez calls itself on this question, this includes the *futuribles* or things which would have taken place had not the opposite come about—for example, the destruction of Ninive, had not people done penance. (Jon 3,5)

there is another reason for this knowledge given by St. Thomas, namely, that God lives in eternity, we in time. Although created things become actual successively, God knows them not successively as we do, but simultaneously. This is because his knowledge is measured by eternity; and eternity, being simultaneously whole, comprises all time. All things are always present to God because his glance reaches from eternity over all things as they are in their actual existence ("presentiality"). Thus it is clear that all things are infallibly known by God inasmuch as they are subject to the divine sight in their presentiality: yet they may be future free acts in relation to their own causes. (*S. Th.* 1ª,14,13) Eternity, as it were, compresses all time, past, present, and future, into the eternal "now."

A VEXING PROBLEM   How can God's absolute knowledge of future free acts be harmonized with man's freedom? If God already knows infallibly that I will act in a certain way, how can I have true freedom of acting otherwise? Does he know how I will act because he determines me to act this way? If so, how am I free? Or does he merely foresee how I will freely choose to act? If so, how is he truly the cause of everything that happens?

This problem has intrigued philosophers and theologians for centuries. Various solutions have been proposed, none fully satisfying. Any solution must start with two basic and undeniable truths: the defined teaching of the Church that man is truly free (D814–816), and the certain teaching that God knows all things, even future free acts of man. Two principal solutions have been advanced: the "Thomist" and the "Molinist," so called. The differences stem from their different viewpoints: the former particularly concerned with vindicating God's total causality, the latter, man's freedom.

The Thomist Solution. This starts with God's total causality of all things. Absolutely nothing can come into existence, including our free thoughts and actions, unless God causes it. He knows it *because* he causes it. By his *knowledge of vision* (*scientia visionis*, i.e., knowledge joined to will) God knows everything that will ever exist. It will exist not merely because it is seen in his essence, but because by the eternal decree of his will he wills that it exist (or in the case of the futurible, that it *not* exist because the opposite happens). By the knowledge of *simple intelligence (scientia simplicis intelligentiae*—i.e., knowledge alone) God knows all the other creatable participations of his essence which in fact will never go beyond mere possibility because they are not included in his eternal decree.

Even a free decision is an entity: it has being, is a perfection. Such cannot be ultimately explained except that God be the cause of it. (*S.C.G.*, 3,68) Thus the created will neither chooses nor is able to choose unless moved to do so by God by what the Thomists call a physical premotion. This motion or determination of the creature is applied in time (*in tempore*), but results from a decree of God that is eternal.

The Thomists are perfectly willing to agree with the Molinists that future free acts are "present" to the eternal gaze of God. But, they say, this presentiality is only explainable in terms of a divine decree. A future free act is a future event from all eternity; therefore it must have a cause from all eternity. But God must be this cause, or else the entity (being) of the choice escapes the divine causality. If the future free act is something good, the decree is one of approbation; if something bad, it is a permissive decree only. By making a sharp distinction between the physical action (which in itself has being and is good) and the moral defect or privation of a sinful act, Thomists insist that God can be the cause of a free and sinful act, but not the cause of the sin. God is cause of the action, but merely permits the defect or formal sin. Since sin is a privation or lack of goodness and being, there is nothing positive about it which would require bringing in God's causality.

By so assiduously defending the divine causality Thomists are naturally charged with endangering human freedom. In their view the future is, so to speak, already determined in advance by God. Without pretending to do away with the mystery, St. Thomas gives what remains the best answer for the Thomist school by simply appealing to the perfection of God's causality, a causality that is so perfect it can bring about events infallibly yet freely. "Since the divine will is of sovereign efficacy, those things which God wishes are not only brought about, but brought about in the manner in which God so wishes," that is, either *necessarily* (e.g., the sun rising tomorrow) or *freely* (e.g., what I will freely choose to do tomorrow). (See *S. Th.*, 1ª,19,18.)

86   *The Molinist Solution.* Luis de Molina (d. 1600), hoping to work out an explanation that will better safeguard human liberty, makes this

liberty his starting point. His explanation, adhered to in some form by nearly all non-Thomists, is based on a third kind of knowledge in God which comes between his knowledge of possibles and his knowledge of actuals. He calls it the "middle knowledge" (*scientia media*).

For Molinists, God's knowledge of future free acts passes, so to speak, through three stages. In the first stage, God knows all creatable things as possibles by the knowledge of simple intelligence, and thus apart from any decree of his will. Merely by knowing himself perfectly, he sees in his essence the infinite possibilities and combinations of things and events, including all free acts that could ever be carried out. This is still in the realm of mere possibility, and would exist even if God had decided never to create anything. Thus for example, he sees what a possible Peter *could* freely choose to do in an infinite variety of circumstances—if created, placed in these circumstances, and given divine help.

In the second stage, and still apart from any decree, God "explores" the *future*, as it were; he infallibly knows all the *future* things by the *scientia media*. (This is the first time that the notion of *future* enters in.) Thus, for example, he knows what Peter, in such or such circumstances and given divine help, *would freely determine to do*. Even now God knows this future because all things are present to him: he sees them in their presentiality, says Molina. Others in this school say rather that he sees them in their objective truth. That is, if it is true that I will act in such or such a way tomorrow, then it was true from eternity, and God who is truth itself could not have been unaware of this bit of truth.

In the third stage, God, by a simple decree of his will, decides to bring into existence the order of things in which are found the circumstances wherein he foresaw that Peter would act freely in a particular way. Thus it is by knowledge plus his decree that God knows what Peter, placed in these circumstances and given divine help, *will actually do*. This absolute future is now the object of the *knowledge of vision*.

Molinists hope by the theory of *scientia media* not only to explain better man's freedom but at the same time to safeguard God's total causality. For, they say, nothing actually exists without his causing it. God brings about the *total* order of the world in which he foresaw certain things would happen. Yet the decree does not bear upon the free determination of human wills, but only on the bringing about of conditions in which God has foreseen such free choices, and upon the divine help (*concursus*) necessary for the effective realization of these free choices.

This theory has the great appeal of apparently safeguarding human liberty (Molina's objective), without denying God's total causality. But its opponents ask—and not without reason—how God can "explore" the future, how there can be any consideration of things as future, unless God causes them to be futures in some way. He cannot know them as any more than mere possibles within his essence, unless some kind of decree of the will relates them to the future. Furthermore, in the theory of the Molinists, the entity of the free choice somehow seems to escape the causality of God.

No theory is entirely satisfactory. Innumerable books have been written on the subject, often generating more heat than light. Ultimately the problem remains a mystery. We must simply remind ourselves of the truths involved—God's total causality and our freedom—and be content with glimpses of how they can be reconciled. Yet strange to say, many people accept the great mystery of the Trinity more readily than this one.

DIVINE VOLITION

To love and desire, to have freedom to act or not act, to choose this instead of that—all these are activities of the will, the faculty that parallels the intellect. The ability to know and choose are the twin glories of man which raise him far above the animal. Just as intelligence is found in God, so also is will. As his act of knowledge is one, perfect, and infinite, so also his act of will.

Scripture

God's will as manifested toward his people is very clear in Scripture. In the act of creating, God gives proof of his will to create. He is portrayed as a God who desires, decides, punishes for disobedience to his commandments. The mission of the prophets is to make known the will of God to man. God has perfect freedom to do what pleases him both in heaven and on earth (Ps 134[135],6); none can resist his will. (Est 13,9)

The New Testament reaffirms that our salvation lies in doing the will of the Father. (Mt 7,21) The most perfect prayer asks that "thy will be done." (Mt 6,10) Jesus himself prays: "Father, if you are willing (if it pleases you), remove this cup from me, yet not my will but yours be done." (Lk 22,42)

Love is the most perfect act of the will, and it is very important to grasp the beautiful scriptural unfolding of God's love toward the human race. For although love is an attribute of God that can be seen even by the philosopher, revelation shows us this same love as an *attitude* of God toward man, a free event whereby God invites us to intimate communion with him; it is a love that is most perfectly seen in and through Christ. Between the Old and New Testaments there is a development not only in man's understanding of God's love, but even in God's loving behavior toward man.

God's love for all things is clearly affirmed in the Old Testament (Wis 11,24) and is a conclusion of natural theology as well. Creation itself is a work of graciousness and goodness. (Ps 135[136],1-9) God's mercy embraces all that he has made. (Ps 144[145],9) Given the fact of creation, this kind of love and mercy is seen as absolutely necessary. It flows from God's nature.

However his *free* love is something else. It sets up the personal "I-Thou" relationship between God and man. This love becomes more and more evident as the story of salvation progresses. God chooses a special people and shows them his love in a personal guidance and protection, sealed by a covenant. He is not deterred by their repeated unfaithfulness, and refuses to abandon them even when they reject him. The psalms and the books of the prophets, particularly, are filled with the realization of this special love, compassion, and readiness to forgive.

Just what the ultimate relationship between God and man is to be is not yet clear in these early writings. Goodness, forbearance, mercy, and solicitude are still attributes or attitudes which can characterize the conduct of a master toward his servant. A *new* relationship is described in the Bible, to be sure: God begins a movement toward man, enters into dialogue with him. The whole thing is already so marvelous that it justifies the image of marital love used, for example, by Osea. This new relationship of love is certainly directed toward the definitive one of the New Testament. For the men of the Old Testament its ultimate tendency is not clear. There, God, as the good and forgiving ruler has not yet indicated that he wishes his servants to have any part or communion with his own personal life. His love is already existential and invites men to personal encounter with him. Man is commanded to love God with his entire being (Dt 6,5); but at this stage God has not yet revealed whether this love is to be the humble love of a servant for his master, or whether it will be the love of adopted sons, involving personal communion with God in the very depths of his inner life. Only the first is evident in the Old Testament. The New Testament gives the answer.

When St. John says "God is love," this is more than a mere statement of an attribute. It is, rather, the only way to express the definitive event of God's free historical behavior toward man. In the fullness of time (Gal 4,4) God communicates his innermost life to men, fully and without restraint. "God so loved the world that he gave his only begotten Son." (Jn 3,16) The incarnation is the ultimate expression of this love. God's total giving of himself through Christ is the definitive plan of God in man's regard; it will never be superseded by any other arrangement. Christ is not only the fullness of revelation but the definitive event of God's love for us. (Rom 8,38)

What is this new relationship of love that comes about through Christ? God gives his very self in Christ. We enter, not into servant-master relations, but into real *fellowship* with his Son Jesus (1 Jn 1,3) and with the Holy Spirit. (2 Cor 13, 13) We are invited to be *children* of God (1 Jn 3,1f), and are called to see him face to face. (1 Cor 13,12) In this way we are taken up into the intimate life of God by being given a share in the very nature of God, with all the rights of sonship; we are *heirs* with Christ, the only-begotten Son. (Rom 8,17.29; Heb. 2,11f)

That God not only loves but is love *is* indeed a conclusion of natural theology about God's attributes. Yet the biblical realization that "God is love" goes far beyond this. It is the expression of the astounding and definitive way in which God has freely offered himself to man in Jesus Christ, the expression of the intimate, personal, and existential love of God for man which the men of the New Testament not only come to know but even *experience* in Christ. (See K. Rahner, *art. cit.,* pp. 118-125.)

90

Theology

OBJECT OF THE DIVINE WILL   The Church is merely confirming
the teaching of Scripture and the Fathers in defining that God is infinite
in intelligence and will, as he is in every perfection. (D1782) But in
this act of his will, what does God will or love, what is the object of his
will act? The *primary* object is himself as infinite goodness or perfection.
There is no egoism involved here, no excessive self-love. The will naturally seeks what is good, and in God is found infinite goodness; God
loves himself infinitely precisely because he is all that is lovable. The
secondary object of God's will is all other things insofar as they partake
of his goodness. (S. Th., 1ª,19,2)

Now it is not difficult to understand that God can exercise his will
in relation to the world, and this in terms of love, anger, power, creation,
justice, mercy, and so on. The only danger is in thinking that God
"changes his mind," when influenced by prayers or events. We must
understand that it is all the result of an eternal act of will which manifests
itself successively from our point of view, and that from all eternity our
free acts and prayers are taken into consideration.

But it is much more difficult to grasp the act of God's will in relation to himself. Even if creatures did not exist, this act of will would
exist. In what does it consist? It consists in the possession of infinite goodness. Just as the divine intellect is not conditioned by creatures, but is
perfectly satisfied by knowing infinite truth, so the divine will, which
seeks goodness, finds its ultimate and final goal in the supreme goodness
which is found in God himself. We cannot really understand this notion
of God knowing and loving himself by an infinite and eternal act of
intellect and will that is identified with his being. Such is demanded
by his simplicity, however, and his essence as self-subsistent being. This
mystery will take on a good deal more interest and cogency in the treatment of the Trinity.

Is God's will free? Not in relation to himself; he wills or loves
himself necessarily. (D1805) The divine will cannot but love what is
infinitely lovable. Moreover, by the very fact that God is, he wills himself, for the divine will is identical with the divine essence. But God
loves other things freely. (S. Th., 1ª,19,3) It cannot be argued that

because love naturally seeks to overflow and communicate itself, God is somehow bound to create in order to bestow goodness on others. (D1805, 3017) Only those things are willed necessarily which are one's goal, or the indispensable means thereto. God, however, is perfect goodness itself: that is goal enough. Creatures are in no way necessary means to this goal. The goodness of God is perfect already and can exist without other things; no perfection accrues to him from created things. Thus he wills created things freely. (*S. Th.*, 1ª,19,2)

DIVISIONS OF THE DIVINE WILL   In order to understand better God's free action with regard to creatures, theologians make certain distinctions in the divine will. There is a solid basis for them in revelation itself, where God has accommodated himself to our limitations in thinking about him. We must remember that in God this will is not divided, nor its act multiplied.

The first division is between God's *will of good pleasure* (*voluntas beneplaciti*) and his *manifested will*. The former is God's true will in relation to us, his will properly speaking. The manifested will is merely the will of God as distinguishable through signs. There are five such signs which in us are accustomed to be taken as signs of another's will. However, not all of them represent God's will of good pleasure. *Operation* (for example, creation itself, the incarnation) always reflects God's true will. *Precept, prohibition,* and *counsel* sometimes coincide with his will of good pleasure, sometimes not. (For example, God's command to Abraham to kill his son Isaac did not, after all, represent God's true will in this case.) Finally, *permission* of sin never corresponds to the will of good pleasure. (*S. Th.*, 1ª,19,11)

A second and more important distinction sees within God's will of good pleasure his *antecedent* and *consequent* will. By his antecedent will, God truly wills that all men worship the one true God, that people honor their parents, live honest lives, and so on. This is his will apart from all complicating circumstances. But we know that this will is not always efficacious, not always carried out. "I called and you refused." (Prv 1,24; also Mt 23,37) We know how often the commandments are broken, and God's will is not done. By his consequent will God wills what actually takes place, causing what is positive, and permitting any moral defects. This is his final will, as it were, in view of all circumstances and considerations. It is this will that is always efficacious, that "none can resist." (Est 13,9) Permission of the evil that takes place is only in view of other circumstances, for example, the greater manifestation of divine mercy, justice, or love. The most striking example of this is God's permission of the sin of Adam, that "happy fault" that brought forth so good and so great a Redeemer.

Justice and Mercy

There are certain affections and moral perfections which people usually attribute to the will. Some of these can be related to God, others cannot. Love, hatred of sin, and joy are properly in God. (S. Th., 1ª, 20) Desire is present only if it denotes the antecedent will that something be done, and wrath only if signifying punishment demanded by justice. Sadness, hope, and fear are too bound up with imperfection, and cannot be harmonized with God's complete happiness and power.

Two perfections are of special interest, justice and mercy. Justice is the will of giving to each one what belongs to him. Now God never owes us anything as equal to equal, for all we have is his (Rom 11,35; 1 Cor 4,7); hence there is no commutative justice in God. But since God is just in rewarding virtue and punishing vice, we can speak of remunerative and vindictive justice in God. (Ps 10[11],7; 34[35],24; Dt 32,41; Rom 12,19; 1 Tim 4,8)

Mercy is the will to come to the prompt relief of others' misery. (S. Th., 1ª,21,3) There seems to be a certain primacy of mercy over justice both in Scripture and in theology because mercy flows more directly from divine goodness, whereas justice presupposes something on man's part, namely good or bad actions. Again, God can be just only because he was first merciful in creating, promising rewards, and granting graces. (Ibid., 4) The theme of mercy is one of the great lessons Christ impressed on his followers: he came not to condemn sinners but to save them. (Mt 9,13; Lk 19,10) If God's saving mercy was heaped upon us even when still sinners, how much more now that we have been reconciled with him through Christ. (Rom 5,8f)

PROVIDENCE, SALVIFIC WILL, PREDESTINATION

Divine Providence

God knew from all eternity that he would create. *Providence* (from *pro-videre*, to foresee) is the plan as conceived in the mind of God for the ordering of the world and all created things to their end. Divine *government*, on the other hand, brings in the divine will: it is the execution of the divine plan, actually establishing this order, putting the plan into effect.

Scripture clearly teaches that God foresees his action in the world; nothing happens by chance. He takes care of his creatures according to his plan. (Wis 8,1; 12,13; 14,3) Mt 6,26ff and I Pet 5,7 show not only the care of God for all things, but a special interest and providence in regard to man. God has even planned that all creatures below man be somehow ordered to man's benefit. (Gn 2)

Belief in God's all embracing providence is part of the Church's faith. (D1784) Nor does the execution of this plan take away the freedom of intellectual creatures in any way, for God arranges all things "beneficently" or "well." (Wis 8,1) God, then, not only is able to bring about what he desires, but is able to bring it about according to the nature of the creature; if the creature has freedom, this freedom is not impaired. Thus the effect of divine providence is not only that things should happen *somehow*, but that they should happen either by necessity or freely. Hence the paradox that not all things which happen infallibly happen necessarily.

God's Universal Salvific Will, or Will to Save All Men

God has planned a supernatural destiny for all men, a life of intimate communion with him in heaven. The ordering of all men to this end, salvation, belongs to the supernatural providence of God. He sincerely wills the salvation of every single person.

94   This loving intent becomes ever clearer in the history of salvation as we find it unfolding in Scripture. Even the Hebrews, who at first think

of God as interested in them alone, finally come to the realization of the love and mercy of God for all mankind, that salvation is for all peoples. (Is 2,2–5; Mal 1,11) In the New Testament, Simeon proclaims the infant Christ as God's salvation prepared for all peoples. (Lk 2,31) This universalism is evident in our Lord's command to the Apostles to teach and baptize all nations. (Mt 28,19f) God does not wish that any should perish (2 Pet 3,9); and St. Paul assures us that Christ gave himself as a ransom for all, and that God "wishes all men to be saved and to come to the knowledge of the truth." (1 Tim 2,4ff)

The Church has had to speak out against the predestinarians, Jansenists, and others who would limit the extent of God's graciousness and Christ's redemption. It is a dogma of faith that God sincerely wills the salvation of all the faithful. (D86, 1096) Though not specifically defined, it is certain that this extends to all adults. (D318) Theologians are likewise agreed that no matter how hard it may be to understand how, God truly wills the salvation even of children who die without baptism.

How does God will the salvation of all, if in fact some are lost? Theologians generally explain that God, by his antecedent will, truly wills the salvation of all, and offers sufficient means to each for salvation. By his consequent will he permits some to be lost, but through their own fault. If he permits this, it is only somehow to make more manifest the divine love and mercy in regard to those who are saved, or the divine justice in the case of those who perish.

Long ago St. John Damascene wrote: "God, by his primary and antecedent will, wishes all men to be saved, and to be partakers of his kingdom. For he did not create us to punish us, but out of goodness, that we might be sharers of his goodness. Yet he wills to punish sinners because of his justice." (*On the Orthodox Faith,* 2,29) Echoing this, the Church declares: "The fact that some are saved is the gift of him who saves; that some perish is the fault of those who perish." (D318)

Predestination

Predestination is a part of divine providence; it is the foreordering or predetermining of the elect to eternal life. That God has a preordained plan of bringing some inevitably to heaven is only hinted at in the Old Testament. (Ex 32,32f; Dn 12,1) But St. Paul gives us a very clear

95

statement: "Those whom God has foreknown he has also predestined to become conformed to the image of his Son, that he should be the firstborn among many brethren. And those whom he has predestined, them he has also called; and those whom he has called, them he has also justified, and those whom he has justified, them he has also glorified." (Rom 8,29f)

The fact of predestination is clearly taught by the Fathers and theologians (e.g., Augustine, *The Gift of Perseverance,* 23,65; St. Thomas, *S. Th.,* 1ᵃ,23,1); and it is defined teaching of the Church. (D805, 825) Knowing that God is the cause of all that happens, we can see that this must be so. God's knowledge and causality do not wait upon the outcome of future events; he is in no way dependent on man's free will. Again, man is absolutely incapable of reaching his goal, heaven, by his own efforts; just as the arrow must be directed and impelled to the target, so man must be directed and helped by God. The plan for bringing men to their eternal goal is called predestination. Execution of this plan will include the things St. Paul mentions: the call to grace, justification, and glorification. Good parents, helpful friends, penance for sin, and many other things can also be looked upon as effects of predestination.

Yet the wonderful mystery is that God does not take away free will in all this. Heaven is a *reward* (Mt 5,12; Rom 2,6; 1 Cor 9,24), and we must freely cooperate with grace. Predestination must not be exaggerated so as to endanger freedom, for both are equally certain facts. The error of the predestinarians was precisely in having man lost or saved without his cooperation, making him a mere plaything of God. (See D816.)

No one can be certain of his own predestination apart from a special revelation from God. (D805, 825, 826) But Scripture tells us that "the Spirit himself gives testimony to our spirit that we are sons of God." (Rom 8,16) And following Ss. Augustine, Anselm, Bernard, and Thomas, theologians teach that there are some signs from which we can conjecture our predestination. These are in part: a good life, readiness to die rather than offend God seriously, patience in difficulties, compassion for the poor, love of enemies, and special devotion to the Holy Spirit, the Blessed Virgin, and the Church.

96

The term predestination is reserved nowadays to this plan of God for the elect. Reprobation, on the other hand, is the will of God permitting some to fall into sin and inflicting the punishment of damnation for sin. (*S. Th.*, 1ª,23,3)

We must not think of reprobation as a predestination to evil. For Scripture is very clear that God wills none to perish. (2 Pet 3,8f) The idea of God *positively* ordering people to damnation is completely out of line with the whole story of salvation, God's love for all, and the universal redemption wrought by Christ. For this reason the Church condemns any who say that God's judgment precedes man's evil deeds (D322), or that God predestines some people to evil by divine power. (D200, 816, 827) As Augustine says: "God can save some without good merits . . . but he cannot damn anyone without evil merits." (*Against Julian*, 3,18,35) St. Fulgentius notes that it would be a still greater injustice if God inflicted punishment on a poor person already predestined to ruin. (*To Monimus*, 1,22) [3]

In the final analysis we cannot escape the conclusion that the reconciliation of divine knowledge and will with human freedom is a mystery which will be understood only in the next life. No philosophical or theological explanation will ever completely satisfy the human mind. The most consoling answer still lies in the evidence of God's love for us as expressed in the person and actions of Christ, and in the loving invitation extended to each to enter into a personal encounter of intimate sonship. Our fate depends upon the free acceptance or refusal of this invitation.

CREATION

The scriptural theme of God's power has already been treated. We know that the Exodus is really the starting point of the Israelite story. The people come to know Yahweh more and more perfectly as they come to a full awareness of his power. At least by the time of the

---

[3] We have omitted the whole controversy as to whether God predestines and reprobates before or after consideration of future merits and demerits. It is a particular application of the Thomist-Molinist controversy over God's foreknowledge and human freedom. A brief sketch would serve only to confuse.

prophets, the almighty power of God is clearly acknowledged. The New Testament, the Fathers, and the earliest creeds all testify to belief in "God the Father almighty." The I Vatican Council is but restating it once more. (D1782)

God's power, then, extends to everything that is intrinsically possible. God can create or do anything that is conceivable, anything that is not a self-contradiction. To ask if God can make a square circle is like asking if he can make a dog that is 100 per cent cat. St. Thomas explains that it is better to say that such "things" are not able to be, than that God cannot make them. (*S. Th.*, 1ª,25,3)

Since God's power is most strikingly evident in the creative act, we shall discuss briefly this evidence of his omnipotence.

Creation in Scripture

Remember that Genesis is not the first book written, though it appears first in the Bible. The account of creation as we have it in Genesis is a composite of two literary traditions: the older, from about 1000 B.C., is the Yahwist tradition represented by Gen 2,4b–25, and the newer, dating from about the seventh century, is the Priestly tradition, represented by Gen 1,1–2,4a. The careful reader will note great differences in these two accounts of creation, the former very simple indeed—barely stating the fact; the latter quite detailed.

The earlier account (starting with 2,4b) says that God "made" (*asah*) the earth and heavens; it is as simple as that. The rest of the account is quite Palestinian: of arid earth quite without life, till God made it rain and brought man into existence to till the soil (2,5f). What the author is really interested in here is the role of man in the original state.

The later account of creation (though prior in the text) is much more systematic and detailed. It is divided into three parts:

(a) 1,1–2 is a short preamble, stating the basic truth of creation. The word used here is "*bara*," meaning a total production in a divine and exceptional way.[4] What is so remarkable in the account is that God,

---

[4] "*Bara*," in the form used here, means total production of the thing under discussion, or production reserved to God: unprecedented phenomena, radical transformations, etc.; e.g., Ex 34,10; Jer 31,22; Is 4.5; 48,7.

simply by the power of his word (1,3ff; cf. Wis 9,1), brings out of primitive chaos the whole hierarchy of being.

(b) 1,3–31 gives a detailed and poetical account of the work of creation over a six-day period. We know today that the author is merely using this as a device or teaching method to get across to his audience the basic fact of the creation of all things by God. The reason for some of the particular divisions and repetitions is probably to serve as a memory device (See B. Vawter, *A Path Through Genesis* [New York: Sheed and Ward, 1955], pp. 31-49.) The author had no more idea than his contemporaries of the details of the divine act of creation so long before. Thus, no argument for or against evolution can be drawn from the creation account in Genesis.

(c) 2,1–4a fixes the limit of creative action. Note that observance of the Sabbath only became law under Moses; but the author is taking the occasion and using this image to impress his listeners with the importance of the Sabbath.

Thus, the over-all account of Genesis on creation gives us the certitude that God's action of bringing all things into existence is creation in the proper sense of the word, although we obviously cannot pretend to see in the word *"bara"* nor in the intention of the author the depth of meaning brought out by later theology.

The prophets (contemporaneous with the two accounts of creation in Genesis) accept the fact of God as author of the world as a traditional certitude. Indeed, they now use the fact of creation as a sort of guarantee of the reality of God's omnipotence. Amos, the oldest of the prophets, recalls the creative omnipotence of Yahweh in warning of his frightful wrath. (4,13; 5,8f; 9,5f) Jeremia does the same thing (51,15ff), but particularly wants to show in the creative act the superiority of Yahweh over all idols. (10,10-16) Isaia uses the fact of creation to inspire both fear and confidence in God. (37,16; also Dt 4,32; 10,14) It is Second Isaia, however, who uses the theme of creation the most. It is for him a sign of God's transcendence. (40,12f; 40,25f) God is sole creator and sole God. (44,24; 45,5ff) This anonymous prophet at the end of the exile proclaims better than anyone else before him the sovereignty of God. God has created everything from the stars to the Gentiles; and in this universality of creation Second Isaia sees the beginning of an action of salvation that is to embrace not only Israel, but all of humanity. (51,6-10)

The Second Book of Machabees, speaks of creation as a "making out of nothing." A mother, forced to watch the torture of her seven sons, encourages them with the thought that God, the creator of the world, who has made the children of her womb, can also restore them in the resurrection. (7,22f) And later she tells the seventh to "look upon heaven and earth and all that is in them: and consider that *God made them out of nothing,* and mankind also." (v. 28) This text is the biblical basis for the theological explanation that creation means a "production from nothing" (*productio ex nihilo*).

St. Paul, in the New Testament, is the only one to add significant details to the biblical account of creation. Creation is a perpetual witness that nothing is impossible to God, and the promise of "him who calls things that are not as though they were" (Rom 4,17) becomes a motive for believing in him. In Romans 1,18–23 (recalling Wis 13, 1–9) Paul assures us that created things proclaim the existence of their Creator. But it not only aids us to get to God by the message it delivers; it *participates* somehow in salvation. The destiny of every creature parallels our own: there is the same groaning under slavery, the same ardent hope in final deliverance. Nature takes part in redemption, and she will take part in the resurrection. (Rom 8,18–25)

Even more striking is Paul's testimony as to the role of Christ in the original creation of the world, and what is more, in its re-creation, or reconciliation with God. All things are made through Christ. (1 Cor 8,6) He is the image of the invisible God, the firstborn of every creature. For in him were created all things in the heavens and on the earth, things visible and invisible. . . . All things have been created through and unto him, and he is before all creatures, and in him all things hold together. . . . For it has pleased God the Father that in him all his fullness should dwell, and that through him he should reconcile to himself all things, whether on the earth or in the heavens, making peace through the blood of the cross." (Col 1,15–20) This beautiful and astounding text presents Christ as the sole, true, and total mediator not only on the religious plane of salvation, but even on the cosmological plane of original creation. Paul is showing us the absolute preeminence of Christ. All has been created in him, takes its coherence from him. He is not "first-born of all creatures" (v. 15) in chronological order, but in the philosophical order. He is the efficient cause, final cause, even exemplary cause of all that exists. He is the meeting-point, the keystone of the universe.

With amazing naturalness Paul injects this cosmological role of Christ into the pattern of his redemptive mission. (Col 1,12–14; 1,18–20) The two mysteries adjoin: the blood of the cross influences the harmony of the world, and Christ in whom is found the fullness of all things reconciles to God everything on earth and in heaven. (1,20; see Eph 1,10)

All this is confirmed by the author of the Epistle to the Hebrews, who speaks of Christ "whom [God] appointed heir of all things, by whom also he made the world; who . . . upholding all things by the word of his power, has brought about man's purgation from sin." (1,2ff)

St. John, in the prologue to his gospel, also speaks of the creative act. But he brings Christ into this act only in his preexistence as the Second Person of the Trinity, the Word. (1,1f) Whether this is all Paul means is a matter of much controversy. It would eliminate the problems raised by having the total Christ involved in creation. But it would also seem to rob the Pauline texts of much of their force and beauty.

Theology of Creation

THE FACT OF CREATION BY GOD ALONE   The creeds affirm belief in "God the Father Almighty, Creator of heaven and earth, of all things visible and invisible." (See D6, 19,54,86.) Creation is the work of God alone. (D1783,1806) No creature could even help in an instrumental way in this unique work, explain the theologians, because an instrument must have something to work upon. But between nonexistence and existence there is no midpoint, no half-finished statue, for example, which the sculptor's chisel can help to shape. And only God can perform the act of bringing something out of nothing. Thus, for example, the worse the soil is, the better a farmer has to be to produce a crop on it; and if the soil is nonexistent it would take a farmer of infinite power to produce the crop. (S. Th., 1ª,45,5; S.C.G. 2, 21–22; De Pot. 3,4)

The creative act is common to the Father, Son, and Holy Spirit, coming from them as from one principle of operation, the divine nature. (D254) Distinctions can be made by way of appropriation—where we attribute (by way of preference, but not exclusion) different parts of the creative work to each person—based on the relation of the persons within the Trinity. Thus, theologians attribute to the Father power, efficient causality, the decree of divine action; to the Son wisdom, exemplary causality, the plan of divine action; and to the Holy Spirit goodness, final causality, the dynamism of the divine action. As we have seen, the role of the Son, the Word of God, is particularly well founded in the writings of St. Paul and St. John. (See also St. Thomas, *On Truth,* 4,8.)

NATURE OF THE CREATIVE ACT   Creation implies an act of intelligence in God. We can speak of "ideas" of created things existing in the mind of God. However, these ideas are not created, nor are they distinct—for there is no composition in God. Rather they are the total idea God has of himself insofar as it is able to be reflected in an infinite variety of finite ways. The divine Word is the supereminent and ever actual expression of all that is imitable in God. This brings out once more the role of the Word as exemplary cause of all things.

Again, creation implies an act of will in God. God has perfect liberty to create or not, and to create this or that thing. We cannot say, strictly speaking, that just because love tends to overflow, God is somehow bound to create. (D1655, 1783, 1805)

God creates out of nothing (*ex nihilo*). This notion—if not the refinements—is implicit in Scripture and the whole of Judeo-Christian thought. (See 2 Mac 7,28; D421, 428.) We are not saying that God uses nothingness as matter out of which he fashions things as from clay; but simply that where there was nothing he causes things to be.[5]

Creation is not an eternal act, not contemporaneous, so to speak, with his eternal activity. Eternal creation is not philosophically impossible; for creatures would still be totally dependent upon God. (S. Th., 1ª,46,2) Modern science is divided: one theory holding the eternity of the universe, the other that it is running down and so must have had a

---

[5] We should not make a real distinction between "creation" and "conservation," as if God finished with the creative act, and is now keeping things going by some different activity. Thus, for example, the source of the river did not create the river and then stop; it constantly creates it. So too God creates the universe, and the universe comes from him unceasingly. St. Thomas reminds us that nothing is able to remain in existence without the continued action of the first cause (S.C.G. 3,65); hence the action which brought things into existence—the creative act—must continue incessantly.

beginning, else it would already have run down. But the creation of things *in time* is clearly a teaching of faith. (Ps 89[90],2; Jn 17,5; Eph 1,4; D428, 501–503,1783)

Neither revelation nor the Church tells us exactly *what* God created in the beginning. Whether it was one immense atom of matter, or nebulous, unformed matter, or already fashioned things, is not important to the doctrine of creation. Creation in the proper sense merely teaches the initial origin of all things from God. All theories of evolution of the world are only involved with a sort of "secondary creation," namely, the modeling of formless or original matter in the present universe.

THE MOTIVE AND PURPOSE OF CREATION   The motive, or what moved God to create, is his Absolute Goodness. "The Lord has made all things for himself." (Prv 16,4) He created, however, not to gain anything for himself, but in order to reflect his perfections in other beings by finite images. The Fathers tell us that God did not create because he needed the world, but in order to "pour out his benefits." (Irenaeus, *Against the Heresies*, 4,14,1) And Augustine says: "We *are* because He is good." (*On Christian Doctrine*, 1,32,35) The I Vatican Council sums this all up in defining that God created "in order to manifest his perfection through the benefits which he bestows on creatures, and not in order to intensify his happiness nor to acquire any perfection." (1783) The aseity and self-subsistence of God, moreover, exclude any extra-divine motive for creation. But we can legitimately speak of a secondary motive for creation, namely, the bestowal of good upon creatures, especially mankind. The I Vatican Council teaches that God created the world "for the manifestation of his perfection" (primary motive) "through the good things which he bestows on creatures" (secondary motive).

The purpose of created things, that is, what they are meant to do, is to give glory to God. Everything, by simply existing, "recounts the glory of God" (Ps 18[19],2); this is called the *objective* glory rendered to God. But even better is that given by intelligent creatures, who can consciously and freely glorify him; this is *formal* glory.

Some have objected that it makes God guilty of egoism to say he intended his own glory to be the purpose of created things. Thus, the Church has had to reaffirm that the world has been created "for the glory of God." (D1805) It is not a question of egoism, after all, but simply of

103

realizing that everything that exists, exists only because of God, and cannot help but be a reflection of him. Creation glorifies God, its author, by being a finite manifestation of his being; any good it has is from him, and its very existence renders striking testimony to the love which brought it into existence. No one who is aware of salvation history can doubt the disinterested love of God in the act of creation. More than just an evidence of his power, creation becomes an act of love opening the door to all the benefits progressively heaped upon mankind by God, culminating in his invitation to personal encounter with him through Christ in this world, and direct, face-to-face union in the next.

Selected Readings

CHAPTERS ONE–THREE

X Bouyer, Louis, *Christian Initiation* (New York: Macmillan, 1960), pp. 21-38.

X Daniélou, Jean, *God and the Ways of Knowing* (New York: Meridian Books, 1957).

X Gelin, Albert, *The Key Concepts of the Old Testament* (New York: Sheed and Ward, 1955), pp. 15-35.

Henry, A. M., *God and His Creation* (Chicago: Fides, 1955), pp. 2-117, 182-195.

Jolivet, Regis, *The God of Reason* (New York: Hawthorn, 1958).

X Lubac, Henri de, *The Discovery of God* (New York: Kenedy, 1960).

Pontifex, Mark, *Freedom and Providence* (New York: Hawthorn, 1960).

X Rahner, Karl, "Theos in the New Testament," *Theological Investigations*, Vol. I (Baltimore: Helicon, 1961), pp. 79-125.

Roberts, David E., *Existentialism and Religious Belief* (New York: Oxford University Press, A Galaxy Book, 1959).

X Tresmontant, Claude, "Biblical Metaphysics," *Cross Currents*, 10 (Summer, 1960), 229-250.

―― *Towards the Knowledge of God* (Baltimore: Helicon, 1961).
Trethowan, Illtyd, *The Basis of Belief* (New York: Hawthorn, 1961).

ABBREVIATIONS

The Books of the Old and New Testaments

Genesis	Gn	Canticle of Canticles	Ct
Exodus	Ex	Wisdom	Wis
Leviticus	Lv	Sirach (Ecclesiasticus)	Sir
Numbers	Nm	Isaia	Is
Deuteronomy	Dt	Jeremia	Jer
Joshua	Jos	Lamentations	Lam
Judges	Jgs	Baruch	Bar
Ruth	Ru	Ezechiel	Ez
1 Samuel (1 Kings)	1 Sm	Daniel	Dn
2 Samuel (2 Kings)	2 Sm	Osea	Os
1 Kings (3 Kings)	1 Kgs	Joel	Jl
2 Kings (4 Kings)	2 Kgs	Amos	Am
1 Chronicles (Paralipomenon)	1 Chr	Abdia	Abd
2 Chronicles (Paralipomenon)	2 Chr	Jona	Jon
Ezra	Ez	Michea	Mi
Nehemia (2 Ezra)	Neh	Nahum	Na
Tobia	Tb	Habacuc	Hb
Judith	Jdt	Sophonia	So
Esther	Est	Aggai	Ag
Job	Jb	Zacharia	Za
Psalms	Ps(s)	Malachia	Mal
Proverbs	Prv	1 Machabees	1 Mc
Coheleth (Ecclesiastes)	Coh	2 Machabees	2 Mc

In the enumeration of the Psalms, the first number follows the Vulgate, the number within brackets, the Hebrew text.

St. Matthew	Mt	1 Timothy	1 Tim
St. Mark	Mk	2 Timothy	2 Tim
St. Luke	Lk	Titus	Ti
St. John	Jn	Philemon	Phlm
Acts of the Apostles	Ac	Hebrews	Heb
Romans	Rom	St. James	Jas
1 Corinthians	1 Cor	1 St. Peter	1 Pt
2 Corinthians	2 Cor	2 St. Peter	2 Pt
Galatians	Gal	1 St. John	1 Jn
Ephesians	Eph	2 St. John	2 Jn
Philippians	Phil	3 St. John	3 Jn
Colossians	Col	St. Jude	Jude
1 Thessalonians	1 Thes	Apocalypse	Ap
2 Thessalonians	2 Thes		

Apocrypha and Qumrân Material

Henoch	Hen	Testament of the	
Jubilees	Jub	Twelve Patriarchs	Test
Psalms of Solomon	Ps Sol	Manual of Discipline	MD

Other Source Material

Acta Apostolicae Sedis
  [Acts of the Apostolic See]   *AAS*
Ancient Christian Writers,
  ed. J. Quasten and others   *ACW*
Acta Sanctae Sedis
  [Acts of the Holy See]   *ASS*
Codex Iuris Canonici
  [Code of Canon Law]   *CIC*
Denzinger-Bannwart, *Enchiridion*
  Symbolorum, 30th ed. [Handbook
  of the Creeds]   *D*
Patrologia, series graeca,
  ed. J. B. Migne   *PG*

Sacrorum Conciliorum nova
  . . . Collectio   *Mansi*
Patrologia, series latina,
  ed. J. B. Migne   *PL*
Summa contra Gentes
  S. Thomae Aquinatis   *S.C.G.*
Quatuor Libri Sententiarum,
  Petri Lombardi [Four Books
  of Opinions]   *Sent.*
Summa Theologiae
  S. Thomae Aquinatis   *S.Th.*
The Church Teaches,
  ed. J. Clarkson and others   *TCT*

INDEX

A

Accident, 73 f
Act, 52, 53, 55
Adonai, 66
Agnostic, 40
Analogy
  of faith, 29
  man's knowledge of God analogous,
    79 f
  notion of, 27-29
Anselm, St., 21, 71, 96
Apostles, 5, 6, 7, 8, 9, 10 f, 12, 13, 14,
    15, 16
  and their grasp of revelation, 10 f, 12,
    13
Aquinas, St. Thomas, 21, 45, 48, 51, 56,
    71, 72, 79, 85, 96
Appropriation, 101 f
Aristotle, 43, 51
Arius, 14
Aseity, 72
Assent, faith as, 18

Assumption of Blessed Virgin, 12
Atheists, 40, 48
Attitudes of God, 82 n.1, 89
Attributes of God
  definition of, 72
  distinctions of, 77
  God as all powerful, 62, 63, 68, 97 f
    eternal, 64, 68, 76
    holy, 67 f
    incomprehensible, 68 f, 78 f
    immanent, 65, 75
    immense, 68 f, 75
    infinite, 69
    infinitely perfect, 74 f
    living, 4, 60 f, 76
    omnipresent, 65, 75
    omniscient, 82
    one, 62 f
    perfect, infinitely, 74 f
    simple, 73, 84
    a spirit, 66 f
    transcendent or completely "other,"
      66 f
    unchangeable, 66, 75 f

B

Bañez, D., 84 n.2
Barth, K., 28 f, 70
Bernard, St., 96
Bible, as soul of theology, 24
    and the Church, 8 f, 25
    and natural knowability of God, 40-44
    and supernatural knowledge of God,
        37 f, 60-68
    and positive theology, 24 f
    and tradition, 5, 6-9
Bishops, 6, 14, 25
Blondel, M., 47
Boethius, 76
Bonaventure, St., 20
Bouyer, L., 36
Buddha, 39 n.1

C

Causality, argument from, 53
    difficulties with, 50 n.4, 55 f
    God's, 86
    God's knowledge by, 86
    principle of, 21
Christ, 4, 5, 7, 8, 9, 10, 14, 15, 17, 18,
        19, 20, 28, 38, 39, 44, 61, 90,
        100 f
    and creation, 100 f
    as culmination of revelation, 4, 5, 7,
        8, 10, 13
    as revealer of God, 38, 61, 90
Church and Bible, 8 f, 24
    as embodiment and preserver of reve-
        lation, 5 f, 7, 9, 10 f, 13, 25
    and natural knowability of God, 45 f
    and nature of God, 68 ff
    as place of encounter, 16, 19
Classic arguments for existence of God,
        51-58
Clement of Alexandria, 20
Commitment, faith as, 16, 17
Comte, A., 45
Concursus, 88
Confucius, 39 n.1
Conscience, argument from, 49
Conservation, 102 n.5
Creation, 72, 97-104
    ex nihilo, 102
    in time, 102 f

Creation (Cont.):
    motive and purpose of, 103
    nature of creative act, 102
    in Scripture, 98-101
    theology of, 101-104
Creator, 46, 62

D

Damascene, St. John, 95
Deism, 75
Desire for happiness, argument from, 49
Development of dogma, 9-14
Dogma, 9-14, 18, 23, 26
Doubt and faith, 16 f

E

Ecumenical Council, 25
Eminence, way of, 79 f
Encounter, 15 f, 17, 38, 61, 70 n.2, 90,
        97, 104
Essence of God, 70 ff, 73 f
Eternity, 64, 68, 76
Existence of God, demonstration of, 56

F

Faith, 15-19, 20 f, 27-29, 38, 61
    and analogy, 27-29
    as encounter, 15 f, 17, 38
    motive of, 19
    object of, 18 f
    and reason, 20 f
Father, God the, 4, 14, 61, 101, 102
Fathers of the Church, 25, 44 f, 73, 83
Fear of the Lord, 67
Fideism, 47, 57
Florence, Council of, 11
Freedom in God, 91, 102
    in man, 50, 85 ff, 94, 96, 97
Fulgentius, St., 97

G

Glory of God, 67, 103
Grace, 16, 17, 57
Grades of being or perfection, argument
        from, 53 f

H

Hegel, G., 68
Heresy, 13, 14, 18
Holiness in God, 67
Holy Spirit, 6, 7, 11, 12, 13, 90, 101
Humani Generis, 56
Hume, D., 45, 55 f

I

Illative sense, 48 n.3
Immaculate Conception, 12
Immanence, 65, 75
Immensity, 68 f, 75
Incomprehensibility of God, 68 f, 78 f
Infallibility, 8, 9, 14, 19, 26
Infinity, 69
Irenaeus, St., 20
Inspiration, 6 f
Intuition of God's existence, 47

J

Jansenists, 95
Jealousy of God, 68
John, St., 20, 24, 101
Justice of God, 91, 93, 95

K

Kant, I., 45, 50, 56, 71
Knowability of God, 36-59
Knowledge in God, 82-88
   by causality, 86
   of futures, 85-88
   by presentiality, 85, 86
Knowledge of vision, 85

L

Leo I, Pope St., 20
Leo XIII, Pope, 24
Lérins, Vincent of, 10
Life in God, 37 f, 60 f, 76
Liturgy and development of dogma, 14,
   25
Lombard, Peter, 20

Love in God, 88-93
   in creating, 104
   object of, 91
   revealed in Christ, 90
Lubac, H. de, 48

M

Magisterium, 6, 14, 25
Majesty of God, 67
Marcel, G., 47, 55, 56, 71
Mary, Blessed Virgin, 12
Mercy, 89, 91, 93, 95
Metaphysical arguments, 51-58
Modernism, 46
Molina, Luis de, 86 f
Molinism, 87, 88
Monotheism, 60, 62 f, 69, 73
Moral arguments for existence of God,
   48-51, 57
Motion, argument from, 51 f
Motive of faith, 19
Mystery, 8, 19, 26, 27
Mystical Body, 5, 6
Mystics, and intuition of God, 47

N

Nature of God, 68, 70 ff
Negation, way of, 79 f
Newman, J. H., 12, 48, 50
Nicea, Council of, 11, 14

O

Object of God's knowledge, 84 f
   of God's love, 91
   of theology, 22
Omnipresence, 65, 75
Omniscience, 82
Order, argument from, 54 f
Origen, 20
Original sin, 39

P

Pagans, 41 f, 62
Pantheism, 68 ff, 74, 75 n.3
Pascal, B., 49, 51

Paul, St., 20, 24, 42 ff, 100 f
Perfection, infinite, 72, 74
Personality in God, 36, 38, 59 f, 77, 79 f
Philosophy, 21
Pius X, Pope St., 46
Pius XII, Pope, 56
Plan of salvation, 4, 5, 8
Plato, 71
Pope, 6, 14, 25
Positive theology, 23-26
Potency, 52, 55
Power of God, 62, 63, 68, 97 f
Predestinarians, 95
Predestination, 95 ff
Presence of God, 4, 65, 75
Protestants, 4, 18
Providence, 72, 94
Providentissimus Deus, 24

R

Rahner, K., 82
Rationalism, 26
Rationalists, 21, 45
Reason and existence of God, 36 f, 39-58
    and faith, 20 f, 26
    and nature of God, 70 ff
    and revelation, 20 f, 26-30, 35 f
Reprobation, 97
Response to God, 5, 15, 17
Revelation, 3, 4, 8, 10, 14, 15, 35-38
    apostles grasp of, 10 f
    and dogma, 10
    and person of Christ, 15
    and reason, 15
    transmission of, 11 ff

S

Salvation, plan of, 4, 5, 8
Scientia media, 87
Scientia simplicis intelligentiae, 86
Scientia visionis, 85, 87 f
Scripture, see Bible
Self-subsistence, 71 f
Semi-rationalism, 26
Simplicity, 73, 84
Skeptic, 40
Socrates, 43
Son of God, 14, 15, 20, 28, 38, 90, 101 f
Sources of revelation, 6 f

Speculative theology, 26-30
Spinoza, 68
Spirituality of God, 66, 67
Substance, 73 f

T

Teaching Church, 6, 14
Theodicy, 22, 59
Theology, 3, 14, 20-30, 35 f
    definition of, 21
    divisions of, 23-30
    light of, 22
    object of, 22
    positive, 23-26
    speculative, 26-30
Thomas Aquinas, St., see Aquinas
Theophilus of Antioch, St., 45
Tradition, 5-8
Traditionalists, 21, 45
Transcendence of God, 66
Trent, Council of, 7, 8, 18
Trinity, 11, 77, 102

U

Unchangeableness of God, 66, 75 f
Unity, 73

V

Vatican, I Council of, 21, 26 f, 46, 68
    74, 75, 78, 83, 103
Volition in God, see Will
Voluntas beneplaciti, 92

W

Will in God, 88-93
    antecedent, 92, 95
    consequent, 92, 95
    divisions of, 92
    of good pleasure, 92
    manifested, 92
    to save all men, 94 f, 97
Word of God, 4, 5, 6, 8 f, 16, 19, 10

Y

Yahweh, 60, 61, 63, 64, 65, 66

Z

Zoroaster, 39 n.1